No god but God

The Origins and Evolution of Islam

No god but God

The Origins and Evolution of Islam

REZA ASLAN

DELACORTE PRESS

Text copyright © 2005 by Reza Aslan
Map © 2011 by Joe LeMonnier
Jacket photographs © 2011 by Patrick Lane/Corbis (top)
and by Mehrdokht Amini (bottom and back)

This work is based upon *No god but God: The Origins, Evolution, and Future
of Islam* by Reza Aslan, published by Random House, an imprint of the
Random House Publishing Group, a division of Random House, Inc.,
New York, in 2005.

Visit us on the Web! www.randomhouse.com/teens
Educators and librarians, for a variety of teaching tools, visit us at
www.randomhouse.com/teachers

Library of Congress Cataloging-in-Publication Data
Aslan, Reza.
No god but God : the origins and evolution of Islam / Reza Aslan.
    p. cm.
Includes index.
ISBN 978-0-385-73975-7 (hardcover) — ISBN 978-0-385-90805-4 (library
binding) — ISBN 978-0-375-89826-6 (ebook) 1. Islam. 2. Islam—Essence,
genius, nature. 3. Islam—History.   I. Title.
BP161.3.A79 2011   297—dc22   2010020408

The text of this book is set in 12-point Adobe Garamond.
Book design by Vikki Sheatsley
Printed in the United States of America
10 9 8 7 6 5 4 3 2 1
First Edition

For my mother, Soheyla,
and my father, Hassan

Contents

1

Religion in Pre-Islamic Arabia

A Brief Word on Prophets and Religion

Prophets do not *create* religions. Because all religions are bound to the social, spiritual, and cultural landscapes from which they arose and in which they developed, prophets must be understood as *reformers* who redefine and reinterpret the existing beliefs and practices of their communities. Indeed, it is most often the prophet's successors who take upon themselves the responsibility of fashioning their master's words and deeds into unified, easily comprehensible religious systems.

Like so many prophets before him, the Prophet Muhammad never claimed to have invented a new religion. On the contrary, by Muhammad's own admission, his message was an attempt to reform the existing religious beliefs and cultural practices of pre-Islamic Arabia so as to bring the God of the Jews and Christians to the Arab peoples. "[God] has established

1

for you [the Arabs] the same religion enjoined on Noah, on Abraham, on Moses, and on Jesus," the Quran says (42:13). It should not be surprising, therefore, that Muhammad would have been influenced as a young man by the religious land-scape of pre-Islamic Arabia. As unique and divinely inspired as the Islamic movement may have been, its origins are un-doubtedly linked to the multiethnic, multireligious society that fed the Prophet's imagination as a young man and al-lowed him to craft his revolutionary message in a language that would have been easily recognizable to the pagan Arabs he was so desperately trying to reach. For whatever else Muhammad may have been, he was, without question, a man of his time. And so, to truly understand the nature and mean-ing of Muhammad's message, we must travel back in time to that intriguing yet ill-defined era of paganism that Muslims refer to as the *Jahiliyyah*—"the Time of Ignorance."

The Time of Ignorance: Arabia, the Sixth Century C.E.

In the arid, desolate basin of Mecca, surrounded on all sides by the bare mountains of the Arabian desert, stands a small, nondescript sanctuary that the ancient Arabs refer to as the *Ka'ba:* the Cube. The Ka'ba is a squat, roofless structure made of unmortared stones and sunk into a valley of sand. Its four walls—so low a young goat could leap over them—are swathed in strips of heavy cloth. At its base, two small doors are chiseled into the gray stone, allowing entry into the inner sanctum. It is here, inside the cramped interior of the sanctu-ary, that the gods of pre-Islamic Arabia reside.

In all, there are said to be three hundred sixty idols housed in and around the Ka'ba, representing every god recognized in the Arabian Peninsula: from the Syrian god Hubal and the powerful Egyptian goddess Isis to the Christian god Jesus and his holy mother, Mary. During the holy months, pilgrims from all over the Peninsula make their way to this barren land to visit their tribal deities. They sing songs of worship and dance in front of the gods; they make sacrifices and pray for health. Then, in a remarkable ritual—the origins of which are a mystery—the pilgrims gather as a group and rotate around the Ka'ba seven times, some pausing to kiss each corner of the sanctuary before being captured and swept away again by the current of bodies.

The pagan Arabs gathered around the Ka'ba believe their sanctuary to have been founded by Adam, the first man. They believe that Adam's original edifice was destroyed by the Great Flood, then rebuilt by Noah. They believe that after Noah, the Ka'ba was forgotten for centuries until Abraham rediscovered it while visiting his firstborn son, Ismail, and his concubine, Hagar, both of whom had been banished to this wilderness at the behest of Abraham's wife, Sarah. And they believe it was at this very spot that Abraham nearly sacrificed Ismail before being stopped by the promise that, like his younger brother, Isaac, Ismail would sire a great nation, the descendants of whom now spin over the sandy Meccan valley like a desert whirlwind.

Of course, these are just stories intended to convey what the Ka'ba *means,* not where it came from. The truth is that no one knows who built the Ka'ba, or how long it has been here. It is likely that the sanctuary was not even the original reason for the sanctity of this place.

It is also possible that the original sanctuary held

3

cosmological significance for the ancient Arabs. Many of the idols in the Ka'ba were associated with the planets and stars; additionally, the legend that they totaled three hundred sixty in number suggests astral connotations. The pilgrims' seven "turnings" around the Ka'ba may have been intended to mimic the motion of the heavenly bodies. It was, after all, a common belief among ancient peoples that their temples and sanctuaries were terrestrial replicas of the cosmic mountain from which creation sprang. The Ka'ba, like the Pyramids in Egypt or the Temple in Jerusalem, may have been constructed as an *axis mundi:* a sacred space around which the universe revolves, the link between the earth and the solid dome of heaven.

Alas, as with so many things about the Ka'ba, its origins are mere speculation. The only thing scholars can say with any certainty is that by the sixth century C.E., this small sanctuary made of mud and stone had become the center of religious life in pre-Islamic Arabia: the time known as Jahiliyyah.

The Pagan Arabs

Traditionally, the Jahiliyyah has been defined by Muslims as an era of moral depravity and religious discord: a time when the sons of Ismail had obscured belief in the one true God and plunged the Arabian Peninsula into the darkness of idolatry. But then, like the rising of the dawn, the Prophet Muhammad emerged in Mecca at the beginning of the seventh century, preaching a message of absolute monotheism and uncompromising morality. Through the revelations he received from God, Muhammad put an end to the paganism of the Arabs and replaced the Time of Ignorance with the universal religion of Islam.

In reality, the religious experience of the pre-Islamic Arabs was far more complex than this tradition suggests. Before the rise of Islam, the Arabian Peninsula was dominated by paganism. But *paganism* is a meaningless and derogatory term created by those outside the tradition to categorize what is an almost unlimited variety of beliefs and practices. The Greek word *paganus* means "a rustic villager" or "a boor," and was originally used by Christians as a term of abuse to describe those who followed any religion but theirs. Unlike Christianity, paganism is a religious perspective that is receptive to a multitude of influences and interpretations. Paganism strives for neither universalism nor moral absolutism.

What's more, it is important to distinguish between the nomadic Bedouin religious experience and the experience of the sedentary tribes that settled in major population centers like Mecca. Bedouin paganism in sixth-century Arabia may have encompassed a range of beliefs and practices, but it was not as concerned with the more metaphysical questions that were cultivated in the larger sedentary societies of Arabia, particularly with regard to issues like the afterlife. The nomadic lifestyle requires a religion to address immediate concerns: Which god can lead us to water? Which god can heal our illnesses?

In contrast, paganism among the sedentary societies of Arabia had developed from its earlier and simpler manifestations into a complex religious tradition, providing a host of divine and semidivine intermediaries who stood between the creator god and his creation. This creator god was called *Allah,* which is not a proper name but a contraction of the word *al-ilah*, meaning simply "the god." Like his Greek counterpart, Zeus, Allah was originally an ancient rain/sky deity who was elevated into the role of the supreme god of the pre-Islamic Arabs. Though a powerful deity to swear by, Allah's eminent status in the Arab pantheon rendered him, like most High Gods, beyond the supplications of ordinary people. It was far more expedient to turn to the lesser, more accessible gods who acted as Allah's middlemen, the most powerful of whom were his three daughters, Allat ("the goddess"), al-Uzza ("the mighty"), and Manat (the goddess of fate). These divine mediators were not only represented in the Ka'ba, they had their own individual shrines throughout the Arabian Peninsula. It was to them that the Arabs prayed when they needed rain, when their children were ill, when they entered into battle or embarked on a journey deep into the treacherous desert.

There were no priests and no pagan scriptures in pre-Islamic Arabia, but the gods regularly revealed themselves through the ecstatic utterances of a group of soothsayers known as the *Kahins*. The Kahins were poets who, for a fee, would fall into a trance in which they revealed divine messages through rhyming couplets. Emerging from every social and economic stratum, and including a number of women, the Kahins interpreted dreams, cleared up crimes, found lost animals, settled disputes, and commented on ethics.

Although called the King of the Gods and the Lord of the House, Allah was not the central deity in the Ka'ba (that honor belonged to the centuries-old Syrian moon god, Hubal). Still, Allah's eminent position in the Arab pantheon is a clear indication of just how far paganism in the Arabian

Peninsula had evolved from its simple animistic roots. One of the most striking examples of this development can be seen in the processional chant that tradition claims the pilgrims sang as they approached the Ka'ba:

Here I am, O Allah, here I am.
You have no partner,
Except such a partner as you have.
You possess him and all that is his.

This proclamation, with its obvious resemblance to the Muslim profession of faith—"There is no god but God"—may reveal the earliest traces in pre-Islamic Arabia of what scholars call *henotheism:* the belief in a single High God, without necessarily rejecting the existence of other, subordinate gods.

Judaism in Pre-Islamic Arabia

Most scholars are convinced that by the sixth century C.E., henotheism had become the standard belief of the vast majority of sedentary Arabs, who not only accepted Allah as their High God, but insisted that he was the same god as Yahweh, the God of the Jews. The Jewish presence in the Arabian Peninsula can, in part, be traced to the Babylonian Exile a thousand years earlier. For the most part, the Jews were a thriving and highly influential community whose culture and traditions had been integrated into the social and religious spheres of pre-Islamic Arabia. Whether Arab converts or immigrants from Palestine, the Jews participated in every level of Arab society. There were Jewish merchants, Jewish Bedouin, Jewish farmers, Jewish poets, and Jewish warriors. Jewish men took Arab names, and Jewish women wore Arab headdresses.

The relationship between the Jews and pagan Arabs was symbiotic in that not only were the Jews heavily Arabized, but the Arabs were also significantly influenced by Jewish beliefs and practices. One need look no further for evidence of this influence than to the Ka'ba itself, whose origin myths indicate that it was a Semitic sanctuary (*haram* in Arabic) with its roots dug deeply in Jewish tradition. Adam, Noah, Abraham, Moses, and Aaron were all in one way or another associated with the Ka'ba long before the rise of Islam, and the mysterious Black Stone that to this day is fixed to the southeast corner of the sanctuary seems to have been originally associated with the same stone upon which the biblical hero Jacob rested his head during his famous dream of the ladder.

The pagan Arab connection to Judaism makes perfect sense when one recalls that, like the Jews, the Arabs considered themselves descendants of Abraham, whom they credited not only with rediscovering the Ka'ba but also with creating the pilgrimage rites that took place there. So revered was Abraham in Arabia that he was given his own idol inside the Ka'ba, as though he were a god himself! That's because in sixth-century Arabia, Jewish monotheism was in no way contrary to Arab paganism. The pagan Arabs would likely have perceived Judaism as just another way of expressing what they considered to be similar religious sentiments.

Christianity in Pre-Islamic Arabia

The same could be said with regard to Arab perceptions of Christianity, which had an influential presence in the Arabian

Peninsula. Between the third and seventh centuries C.E., Arabia was in the foreground of the wars between the Christian empires of Rome and Byzantium and the Sasanian (Persian) Empire. By the sixth century C.E., Yemen had become the seat of Christian aspirations in Arabia; the city of Najran was widely considered to be the hub of Arab Christianity, while in Sana', a massive church had been constructed that, for a time, vied with Mecca as the primary pilgrimage site in the region. As a proselytizing faith, Christianity did not remain at the borders of the Arab lands. A number of Arab tribes had converted en masse to Christianity. The largest of these tribes was the Ghassanids, who straddled the border between the Roman and Byzantine empires and the Arab worlds. The Ghassanids actively supported missionary efforts in Arabia, while at the same time the Byzantine emperors sent their bishops deep into the deserts to bring the rest of the pagan Arabs into their fold.

Christianity's presence in the Arabian Peninsula likely had a significant effect on the pagan Arabs. (According to the traditions, the image of Jesus residing in the sanctuary had been placed there by a Coptic Christian named Baqura.) It has often been noted that the biblical stories recounted in the Quran imply a familiarity with the traditions and narratives of the Christian faith. There are striking similarities between the Christian and Quranic descriptions of the Apocalypse, the Last Judgment, and the paradise awaiting those who have been saved. These similarities do not contradict the Muslim belief that the Quran was divinely revealed, but they do indicate that the Quranic vision of the Last Days may have been revealed to the pagan Arabs through a set of symbols and metaphors with which they were already familiar, thanks in some part to the wide spread of Christianity in the region.

Zoroastrianism's Influence in Pre-Islamic Arabia

While the Ghassanids protected the borders of the Byzantine Empire, another Arab tribe, the Lakhmids, provided the same service for the Sasanian Empire. As the imperial inheritors of the ancient Persian kingdom of Cyrus the Great, which had dominated Central Asia for nearly a millennium, the Sasanians were Zoroastrians, followers of the ancient prophet Zarathustra.

At the center of Zoroastrian theology was a unique monotheistic system based on the sole god, Ahura Mazda ("the Wise Lord"). Like most ancients, Zarathustra could not easily conceive of his god as being the source of both good and evil. He therefore developed an ethical dualism in which two opposing spirits, *Spenta Mainyu* ("the beneficent spirit") and *Angra Mainyu* ("the hostile spirit"), were responsible for good and evil, respectively.

Although these two spirits were not gods but only the spiritual embodiment of Truth and Falsehood, by the time of the Sasanians, Zarathustra's early monotheism had transformed into a *dualistic* system in which the two primordial spirits became two deities locked in an eternal battle for the souls of humanity: Ohrmazd, the God of Light, and Ahriman, the God of Darkness. Despite being a nonproselytizing and notoriously difficult religion to convert to, the Sasanian military presence in the Arabian Peninsula had nonetheless resulted in a few tribal conversions to Zoroastrianism.

Hanifism in Pre-Islamic Arabia

The picture that emerges from this brief outline of the pre-Islamic Arabian religious experience is that of an era in which Zoroastrianism, Christianity, and Judaism intermingled in one of the last remaining regions in the Near East still dominated by paganism. The relative distance that these three major religions enjoyed from their respective centers gave them the freedom to develop their own creeds and rituals. In Mecca, the vibrant pluralistic environment became a breeding ground for bold new ideas and exciting religious experimentation, the most important of which was an obscure Arab monotheistic movement called *Hanifism,* which arose some time around the sixth century C.E.

The legendary origins of Hanifism are recounted in the writings of one of Muhammad's earliest biographers, Ibn Hisham. One day, while the Meccans were celebrating a pagan festival at the Ka'ba, four men—Waraqa ibn Nawfal, Uthman ibn Huwairith, Ubayd Allah ibn Jahsh, and Zayd ibn Amr—met secretly in the desert. They agreed, "in the bonds of friendship," that they would never again worship the idols of their forefathers. They made a solemn pact to return to the unadulterated religion of Abraham, whom they considered to be neither a Jew nor a Christian but a pure monotheist: a *hanif* (from the Arabic root *hnf,* meaning "to turn away from," as in one who turns away from idolatry). The four men left Mecca and went their separate ways, preaching the new religion and seeking out others like them. In the end, Waraqa, Uthman, and Ubayd Allah all converted to Christianity, but Zayd continued in the new faith. Despite

11

his call for monotheism and his repudiation of the idols inside the sanctuary, Zayd maintained a deep veneration for the Ka'ba itself, which he believed was spiritually connected to Abraham. "I take refuge in that in which Abraham took refuge," Zayd declared.

By all accounts, the Hanif movement flourished throughout western Arabia, or the *Hijaz,* especially in major population centers. It is impossible to say how many Hanif converts there were in pre-Islamic Arabia, or how large the movement had become. What seems evident, however, is that there were many in the Arabian Peninsula who were actively struggling to transform the vague henotheism of the pagan Arabs into a distinctly Arabian form of monotheism.

Hanifism was, like Christianity, a proselytizing faith, so its ideology would have spread throughout the Hijaz. Most sedentary Arabs would have heard Hanif preachers; the Meccans would surely have been familiar with Hanif ideology; and there can be little doubt that the Prophet Muhammad would have been aware of both.

2

The World into Which Muhammad Was Born

The Tribal Ethic

For the Bedouin, the only way to survive in a community in which movement was the norm and material accumulation impractical was to maintain a strong sense of tribal solidarity by evenly sharing all available resources. Thus, every member of the tribe had an essential function in maintaining the tribe's stability, and the tribe itself was only as strong as its weakest members. That's where the tribal ethic came in. Its purpose was to maintain a semblance of social egalitarianism so that, regardless of one's position, every member could share in the social and economic rights and privileges that preserved the unity of the tribe.

In pre-Islamic Arabia, the responsibility for maintaining the tribal ethic fell upon the *Sayyid*, or *Shaykh*, of the tribe. Unanimously elected as "the first among equals," the Shaykh, which means "one who bears the marks of old age," was the most highly respected member of his community, the figurehead who represented the strength and moral attributes of the tribe. Although it was a common belief that the qualities of leadership and nobility were inherent in certain families, the Shaykh was not a hereditary position. The only requirement for becoming a Shaykh, besides maturity, was to embody the ideals of *muruwah:* the code of tribal conduct that was composed of important Arab virtues like bravery, honor, hospitality, strength in battle, concern for justice, and, above all, an assiduous dedication to the collective good of the tribe.

The Shaykh had little real executive authority because the Arabs were wary of concentrating all the functions of leadership in a single individual. Every important decision was made through collective consultation with other individuals in the tribe who had equally important roles: the *Qa'id,* who acted as war leader; the *Kahin,* or cultic official; and the *Hakam,* who settled disputes. The Shaykh may occasionally have acted in one or more of these functions, but his primary responsibility was to maintain order within and between the tribes by assuring the protection of every member of his community, especially those who could not protect themselves: the poor and the weak, the young and the elderly, the orphan and the widow. Loyalty to the Shaykh was symbolized by an oath of allegiance called *bay'ah,* which was given to the man, not to the office. If the Shaykh failed in his duty to adequately protect every member of his tribe, the oath would be withdrawn and another leader chosen to fill his place.

In a society with no concept of an absolute morality as dictated by a divine code of ethics—a Ten Commandments, if you will—the Shaykh had only one legal recourse for maintaining order in his tribe: the Law of Retribution, more popularly known as the somewhat crude concept of "an eye for an eye." Far from being a barbaric legal system, the Law of Retribution was actually meant to limit barbarism. Accordingly, an injury to a neighbor's eye confined retaliation to *only an eye and nothing more;* the theft of a neighbor's camel required payment of exactly one camel; killing a neighbor's son meant the execution of one's own son. To facilitate retribution, a pecuniary amount, known as "blood money," was established for all goods and assets as well as for every member of society and, in fact, for every part of an individual's body. In Muhammad's time, the life of a free man was worth about one hundred camels; the life of a free woman, fifty.

It was the Shaykh's responsibility to maintain peace and stability in his community by ensuring the proper retribution for all crimes committed within the tribe. Crimes committed against those *outside* the tribe were not only unpunished, they were not really crimes. Stealing, killing, or injuring another person was not considered a morally reprehensible act per se; such acts were punished only if they weakened the stability of the tribe.

Occasionally, the sense of balance inherent in the Law of Retribution was skewed because of some logistical complication. For example, if a stolen camel turned out to be pregnant, would the thief owe the victim one camel or two? Because there was no formal law enforcement and no judicial system at all in tribal societies, in cases requiring negotiation, the two sides would bring their arguments to a Hakam: any trusted neutral party who acted as an arbiter in the dispute. After collecting a security from both sides to ensure that all parties would abide by his arbitration—which was, technically, unenforceable—the Hakam would make an authoritative legal declaration: "A pregnant camel is worth two camels." As the Hakam's arbitrations accumulated over time, they became the foundation of a normative legal tradition, or *Sunna,* that served as the tribe's legal code. In other words, never again was arbitration needed to decide the worth of a pregnant camel.

However, because each tribe had its own Hakams and its own Sunna, the laws and traditions of one tribe did not necessarily apply to another. It was often the case that an individual had no legal protection, no rights, and no social identity whatsoever outside his own tribe. How the pre-Islamic Arabs were able to maintain intertribal order when there was technically nothing *morally* wrong with stealing from, injuring, or killing someone outside one's own tribe is a complicated matter. The tribes maintained relationships with one another through a complex network of alliances and affiliations. But the easy answer is that, if someone from one tribe harmed a member of another, the injured tribe, if strong enough, could demand retribution. Consequently, it was the Shaykh's responsibility to ensure that neighboring tribes understood that any act of aggression against his people would be equally avenged. If he could not provide this service, he would no longer be Shaykh.

The Quraysh

The Quraysh were the most powerful and wealthy of the Bedouin tribes that had settled in Mecca. Known throughout the Hijaz as *ahl Allah:* "the Tribe of God," the Wardens of the Sanctuary, the Quraysh's dominance of Mecca began at the end of the fourth century C.E., when an ambitious young man named Qusayy gained control of the Ka'ba by uniting a number of feuding clans under his rule. Clans in the Arabian Peninsula were primarily composed of large extended families that called themselves either *bayt* (house of) or *banu* (sons of) the family's patriarch. Muhammad's clan was thus known as Banu Hashim, "the Sons of Hashim." Through intermarriage and political alliances, a group of clans could merge to become an *ahl* or a *qawm:* a "people," more commonly called a tribe.

Qusayy's genius was his recognition that the source of Mecca's power rested in its sanctuary; simply put, he who controlled the Ka'ba controlled the city. By appealing to the ethnic sentiments of his Qurayshi kinsmen, whom he called "the noblest and purest of the descendants of Ismail," Qusayy was able to capture the Ka'ba from his rival clans and declare himself King of Mecca. Although he allowed the pilgrimage rituals to remain unchanged, he alone held the keys to the temple. As a result, he had sole authority to feed and provide water to the pilgrims, to preside at assemblies around the Ka'ba where marriage and circumcision rites were performed, and to hand out the war banners. As if to emphasize further the sanctuary's power to bestow authority, Qusayy divided Mecca into quarters, creating an outer and an inner ring of settlements. The closer one lived to the sanctuary, the greater one's power. Qusayy's house was actually attached to the Ka'ba.

The significance of Qusayy's proximity to the sanctuary was not lost on the Meccans. It would have been difficult to ignore the fact that the pilgrims who circled around the Ka'ba were also circling around Qusayy. And because the only way to enter the Ka'ba's inner shrine was through a door located

17

inside Qusayy's house, no person could approach the gods in the sanctuary without first going through Qusayy. In this way, he bestowed upon himself both political and religious authority over the city. He was not just the King of Mecca, he was the Keeper of the Keys.

Qusayy's most important innovation was the establishment of what would become the foundation of Mecca's economy. He began by strengthening his city's position as the dominant place of worship in the Hijaz, collecting all the idols venerated by neighboring tribes and transferring them to the Ka'ba. Henceforth, if one wanted to worship, say, the lover gods, Isaf and Na'ila, one could do so only at Mecca, and only after paying a toll to the Quraysh for the right to enter the sacred city. As Keeper of the Keys, Qusayy also maintained a monopoly over the buying and selling of goods and services to the pilgrims, which he in turn paid for by taxing the city's inhabitants and keeping the surplus for himself. In a few short years, Qusayy's system had made him—and those ruling clans of Quraysh who had managed to connect their fortunes with his—enormously wealthy. But there was even more profit to be made in Mecca.

Like all Semitic sanctuaries, the Ka'ba transformed the entire surrounding area into sacred ground, making the city of Mecca a neutral zone where fighting among tribes was prohibited and weapons were not allowed. The pilgrims who traveled to Mecca during the pilgrimage season were encouraged to take advantage of the peace and prosperity of the city by bringing with them merchandise to trade. To facilitate this, the great commercial fairs coincided with the pilgrimage cycle, and the rules for one complemented those for the other. A few generations after Qusayy, under the directive of his grandson and Muhammad's great-grandfather, Hashim, the Quraysh had managed to create a modest but lucrative trading zone in Mecca, one which relied almost entirely on the Ka'ba's pilgrimage cycle for its subsistence.

Because every god in pre-Islamic Arabia was said to reside in the Ka'ba, all peoples of the Arabian Peninsula, regardless of their tribal beliefs, felt a deep spiritual obligation not only to this single sanctuary but also to the city that housed it and the tribe that preserved it. By linking the religious and economic life of the city, Qusayy and his descendants had developed an innovative religio-economic system that relied on control of the Ka'ba and its pilgrimage rites to guarantee the economic, religious, and political supremacy of a single tribe: the Quraysh.

3

Muhammad in Mecca

Birth of Muhammad

Muhammad was born, according to Muslim tradition, in 570 C.E., the same year that Abraha, the Christian Abyssinian ruler of Yemen, attacked Mecca with a herd of elephants in an attempt to destroy the Ka'ba and make the church at Sana' the new religious center in the Arabian Peninsula.

In a society with no fixed calendar, the Year of the Elephant, as it came to be known, was not only the most important date in recent memory, it was the commencement of a new Arab chronology. That is why the early biographers set Muhammad's birth in the year 570, so that it would coincide with another significant date. But 570 is neither the correct year of Muhammad's birth nor of the Abyssinian attack on Mecca; modern scholarship has determined that momentous event to have taken place around 552 C.E.

20

The fact is that no one knows now, just as no one knew then, when Muhammad was born, because birthdays were not necessarily significant dates in pre-Islamic Arab society. Muhammad himself may not have known in what year he was born. In any case, nobody would have cared about Muhammad's birth date until long after he was recognized as a prophet, perhaps not even until long after he had died. Only then would his followers have wanted to establish a year for his birth in order to institute a firm Islamic chronology. And what more appropriate year could they have chosen than the Year of the Elephant? For better or worse, the closest our modern historical methods can come to determining the date of Muhammad's birth is some time in the last half of the sixth century C.E.

The Young Muhammad

As an infant, Muhammad was placed in the care of a Bedouin foster mother to be nursed, a common tradition among Arabs of sedentary societies who wanted their children to be raised in the desert according to the ancient customs of their forefathers. Appropriately, it was in the desert that Muhammad had his first prophetic experience.

According to tradition, while herding a flock of lambs, he was approached by two men clothed in white, who carried with them a golden basin full of snow. The two men came to Muhammad and pinned him to the ground. They reached into his chest and removed his heart. After extracting a drop of black liquid from it, they washed the heart clean in the snow and gently placed it back into Muhammad's breast before disappearing.

When Muhammad was six years old, his mother died (his father had died before he was born), and he was sent to live with his grandfather Abd al-Muttalib, who filled one of the most influential pagan posts in Meccan society, the man in charge of providing the pilgrims with water from a nearby well called Zamzam. Two years later, Abd al-Muttalib also died, and the orphaned Muhammad was once again shuttled off to another relative, this time to the house of his powerful uncle, Abu Talib. Taking pity on the boy, Abu Talib employed Muhammad in his lucrative caravan business. It was during one of these trading missions, while the caravan made its way to Syria, that Muhammad's prophetic identity was finally revealed.

Abu Talib had prepared a large trading expedition to Syria, when he decided, at the last moment, to take Muhammad along. As the caravan moved slowly across the scorched landscape, a Christian monk named Bahira caught sight of it passing by his monastery at Basra.

Bahira possessed a secret book of prophecy passed down from generation to generation by the monks in his order. He had pored over the ancient manuscript and discovered within its weathered pages the coming of a new prophet. It was for this reason that he decided to stop the caravan. Bahira noticed that as the convoy balanced its way over the thin gray horizon, a small cloud hovered continuously over one member of the group, shielding only him from the heat of the merciless sun. When this person stopped, so did the cloud; and when he dismounted his camel to rest under a tree, the cloud followed him, overshadowing the tree's meager shade until its slender branches bent down to shelter him.

Recognizing what these signs could mean, Bahira sent an

22

urgent message to the caravan leaders. "I have prepared food for you," the message read. "I should like you all to come, both great and small, bond and free."

The members of the caravan were startled. They had passed the monastery many times on their way to Syria, but Bahira had never before taken notice of them. Nevertheless, they decided to break for the evening and join the old monk. As they ate, Bahira noticed that the one he had seen in the distance, the one who was attended by the clouds and the trees, was not among them. He asked the men if every member of the caravan was present. "Do not let any of you remain behind and not come to my feast."

The men replied that everyone who ought to be present was present, except, of course, the young boy, Muhammad, whom they had left outside to watch over the baggage. Bahira was elated. He insisted the boy join them. When Muhammad entered the monastery, the monk gave him a brief examination and declared to everyone present that this was the Messenger of the Lord of the Worlds. Muhammad was nine years old.

If the childhood stories about Muhammad sound familiar, it is because they function as what scholars call a prophetic *topos:* a conventional literary theme that can be found in most mythologies. Like the infancy narratives in the Gospels, these stories are not intended to relate historical events but to shed light on the mystery of the prophetic experience. They answer the questions: What does it mean to be a prophet? Does one suddenly become a prophet, or is prophethood a state of existence established before birth, indeed before the beginning of time? If the latter, then there must have been signs foretelling the prophet's arrival: a miraculous conception, perhaps, or some prediction of the prophet's identity and mission.

23

Still, when combined with what is known about pre-Islamic Arab society, one can glean important historical information from these stories. For example, we can reasonably conclude that Muhammad was a Meccan and an orphan; that he worked for his uncle's caravan from a young age; that this caravan made frequent trips throughout the region and would have encountered Christian, Zoroastrian, and Jewish tribes, all of whom were deeply involved in Arab society; and finally, that he must have been familiar with the religion and ideology of Hanifism, which pervaded Mecca and which very likely set the stage for Muhammad's own challenge to the pagan authorities who controlled the holy city.

Muhammad in Meccan Society

The concentration of wealth in the hands of a few ruling families in Mecca had not only altered the social and economic landscape of the city, it had effectively destroyed the tribal ethic and swept away tribal ideals of social egalitarianism. No longer was there any concern for the poor and marginalized; no longer was the tribe only as strong as its weakest members. The Shaykhs of the Quraysh had become far more interested in their personal wealth and in maintaining the apparatus of trade than in caring for the dispossessed.

With the demise of the tribal ethic, Meccan society became strictly stratified. At the top were the leaders of the ruling families of Quraysh. If one was fortunate enough to acquire enough capital to start a small business, one could take full advantage of the city's religio-economic system. But for most Meccans, this was simply not possible. Especially for those with no formal protection—such as orphans and widows, neither of whom had access to any kind of inheritance—the only option was to borrow money from the rich at exorbitant interest rates, which inevitably led to debt, which in turn led to crushing poverty and, ultimately, to slavery.

As an orphan, Muhammad understood the difficulty of falling outside Mecca's religio-economic system. Fortunately for him, his uncle and new guardian, Abu Talib, was also the Shaykh of the Banu Hashim—a small, not very wealthy, yet prestigious clan within the mighty tribe of Quraysh. It was Abu Talib who kept Muhammad from falling into the debt and slavery that were the fate of so many orphans in Mecca, by providing him with a home and the opportunity to eke out a living working for his caravan.

There is no question that Muhammad was good at his job. The traditions go to great lengths to emphasize his success as a skillful merchant who knew how to strike a lucrative deal. Despite his lowly status in Meccan society, he was widely known throughout the city as an upright and pious man. His nickname was *al-Amin,* "the trustworthy one," and he was on a few occasions chosen to serve as Hakam in small disputes.

As honest or skilled as he may have been, by the turn of the seventh century, Muhammad was a twenty-five-year-old man still unmarried, with no capital and no business of his own, who relied entirely on his uncle's generosity for his employment and his housing. In fact, his prospects were so depressingly low that when he asked for the hand of his uncle's daughter, Umm Hani, she rejected him outright for a more prosperous suitor.

Things changed for Muhammad when he attracted the attention of a remarkable forty-year-old widow named Khadija. A wealthy and respected female merchant in a society that treated women as chattel and prohibited them from inheriting the property of their husbands, Khadija managed to become one of the most respected members of Meccan society. She owned a thriving caravan business and was pursued by many men, most of whom would have loved to get their hands on her money.

According to the historian Ibn Hisham, Khadija first met Muhammad when she hired him to lead one of her caravans. She had heard of his "truthfulness, reliability, and nobility of character" and decided to entrust him with a special expedition to Syria. Muhammad returned from the trip with almost double the profits Khadija had expected, and she rewarded him with a proposal of marriage.

Muhammad's marriage to Khadija paved the way for his acceptance at the highest levels of Meccan society and thoroughly initiated him into the religio-economic system of the city. By all accounts, he was extremely successful in running his wife's business, rising in status and wealth until he was, while not part of the ruling elite, a member of what may be considered anachronistically "the middle class."

Muhammad's Early Revelations

Despite his success, Muhammad felt deeply conflicted by his dual status in Meccan society. On the one hand, he was renowned for his generosity and the evenhandedness with which he conducted his business. Although now a well-respected and relatively affluent merchant, he frequently went on solitary retreats of "self-justification," the pagan practice known as *tahannuth,* in the mountains and glens surrounding the Meccan valley, and he regularly gave money and food to the poor in a religious charity ritual tied to the cult of the Ka'ba. On the other hand, he seemed to be acutely aware of his complicity in Mecca's religio-economic system, which exploited the city's unprotected masses in order to maintain the wealth and power of the elite. For fifteen years he struggled with the incongruity between his lifestyle and his beliefs; by his fortieth year, he was an intensely troubled man.

Then, one night in 610 C.E., as he was meditating on Mount Hira during one of his religious retreats, Muhammad had an encounter that would change the world.

He sat alone in a cave, deep in meditation. Suddenly, an invisible presence crushed him in its embrace. He struggled to break free but could not move. He was overwhelmed by darkness. The pressure in his chest increased until he could no longer breathe. He felt he was dying. As he surrendered his final breath, light and a terrifying voice washed over him "like the break of dawn."

"Recite!" the voice commanded.

"What shall I recite?" Muhammad gasped.

The invisible presence tightened its embrace. "Recite!"

"What shall I recite?" Muhammad asked again, his chest caving in.

Once more the presence tightened its grip and once more the voice repeated its command. Finally, at the moment when he thought he could bear no more, the pressure in his chest stopped, and in the silence that engulfed the cave, Muhammad felt these words stamped upon his heart:

Recite in the name of your Lord who created,
Created humanity from a clot of blood.
Recite, for your Lord is the Most Generous One

Who has taught by the pen,
Taught humanity that which it did not know. (96:1–5)

This was Muhammad's burning bush: the moment in which he ceased being a Meccan businessman concerned with society's ills and became what in the Abrahamic tradition is called *prophet*. Yet, like his great prophetic predecessors— Abraham, Moses, David, and Jesus—Muhammad would be something more.

Muslims believe in the continual self-revelation of God from Adam down to all the prophets who have ever existed in all religions. These prophets are called *nabi* in Arabic, and they have been chosen to relay God's divine message to all humanity. But sometimes a nabi is given the extra burden of handing down sacred texts: Moses, who revealed the Torah; David, who composed the Psalms; Jesus, whose words inspired the Gospels. Such an individual is more than a mere prophet; he is God's messenger—a *rasul*. Thus, Muhammad the merchant from Mecca, who over the course of the next twenty-three years will recite the entire text of the Quran (literally, "the Recitation"), would henceforth be known as *Rasul Allah:* "the Messenger of God."

What that first experience of Revelation was like for Muhammad is difficult to describe. The sources are vague, sometimes conflicting. Ibn Hisham states that Muhammad was sleeping when the Revelation first came to him like a dream, while al-Tabari claims the Prophet was standing when the Revelation dropped him to his knees; his shoulders trembled and he tried to crawl away. The command (*iqra*) that Muhammad heard in the cave is best understood as "recite" in al-Tabari's biography but is clearly intended to mean "read" in

Ibn Hisham's. In fact, according to one of Ibn Hisham's traditions, the first recitation was actually written on a magical brocade and placed in front of Muhammad to be read.

Muslim tradition focuses on al-Tabari's definition of *iqra* ("recite"), mostly to emphasize the notion that the Prophet was illiterate, which some say is validated by the Quran's epithet for Muhammad: *an-nabi al-ummi,* traditionally understood as meaning "the unlettered Prophet." But while Muhammad's illiteracy may enhance the miracle of the Quran, there is no historical justification for it. As many Arabic scholars have demonstrated, *an-nabi al-ummi* should more properly be understood as "the Prophet for the unlettered" (that is, the Scriptureless), a translation consistent both with the grammar of the sentence and with Muhammad's view that the Quran is the Revelation for a people without a sacred book: "We did not give [the Arabs] any previous books to study, nor sent them any previous Warners before you" (34:44).

The fact is that it would be highly unlikely for a successful merchant like Muhammad to have been unable to read and write the receipts of his own business. Obviously, he was neither a scribe nor a scholar, and he in no way had the verbal prowess of a poet. But he must have been able to read and write basic Arabic—names, dates, goods, services—and, considering that many of his customers were Jews, he may even have had rudimentary skills in Aramaic.

The traditions also disagree about how old Muhammad was when the Revelation first came to him: Some chroniclers say forty; others claim he was forty-three. Although there is no way to know definitively, the scholar Lawrence Conrad notes that it was a common belief among the ancient Arabs that "a man only reaches the peak of his physical and intellectual powers when he becomes forty years old." The Quran confirms this belief by equating manhood with the realization of the fortieth year of life (46:15). In other words, the ancient biographers may have been guessing when they attempted to calculate Muhammad's age at Mount Hira, just as they were probably guessing when they figured the year of his birth.

Likewise, there is a great deal of confusion over the precise date of that first revelatory experience. It is cited as having occurred either on the fourteenth, seventeenth, eighteenth, or twenty-fourth day of the month of Ramadan. There is even some debate within the earliest community over exactly what the first recitation was: Some chroniclers claim that God's first command to Muhammad was neither "recite" nor "read" but rather "arise and warn!"

Perhaps the reason the traditions are so vague and conflicting is that there was no single momentous revelatory event that initiated Muhammad's prophethood but rather a series of smaller, indescribable supernatural experiences that climaxed in a final, violent encounter with the Divine. Aisha, who would become the Prophet's closest and most beloved companion, claimed that the first signs of prophethood occurred long before the experience at Mount Hira. These signs came in the form of visions that assailed Muhammad in his dreams, and which were so disturbing that they made him increasingly seek solitude. "He liked nothing better than to be alone," Aisha recalled.

Muhammad's disturbing visions seem to have been accompanied by aural perceptions. Ibn Hisham records that when the Prophet set off to be alone in the "glens of Mecca," the stones and trees that he passed along the way would say, "Peace unto thee, O Apostle of Allah." When this happened, Muhammad "would turn to his right and left and look behind him and he would see naught but trees and stones." These aural and visual hallucinations continued right up to the moment in which he was called by God at Mount Hira.

It seems certain that Muhammad, like all the prophets before him, wanted nothing to do with God's calling. So despondent was he about the experience that his first thought was to kill himself.

As far as Muhammad understood, only the Kahin, whom he despised as reprehensible charlatans, received messages from the heavens. If his experience at Mount Hira meant that he was himself becoming a Kahin and that his colleagues in Mecca were now going to regard him as such, then he would rather be dead.

Muhammad was right to worry about being compared to a Kahin. What is impossible to discern in any translation of those first few verses of the Revelation is their exquisite poetic quality. That initial recitation, and those immediately following, were delivered in rhyming couplets that were very much like the ecstatic utterances of the Kahin. This would not have been unusual; after all, the Arabs were used to hearing the gods speak in poetry, which elevated their language to the realm of the divine. But much later, when Muhammad's message began to clash with the Meccan elite, his enemies would seize upon the similarities between the oracles of the Kahin and Muhammad's recitations, asking mockingly: "Should we abandon our gods for the sake of an insane poet?" (37:36)

The fact that there are dozens of verses in the Quran refuting the accusation that Muhammad was a Kahin indicates how important the issue was for the early Muslim community. As Muhammad's movement expanded throughout the region, the Revelation gradually became more prosaic and ceased to resemble the oracular style of the early verses. However, in the beginning, Muhammad knew exactly what would be said of him, and the thought of being considered a Kahin by his contemporaries was enough to bring him to the edge of suicide.

Eventually, God relieved Muhammad's anxiety by assuring him of his sanity. But it is safe to say that if it were not for Khadija, Muhammad might have gone through with his plan to end it all, and history would have turned out quite differently.

"By her, God lightened the burden of His prophet," Ibn Hisham writes of the remarkable Khadija. "May God Almighty have mercy upon her!"

Still frightened and trembling from the experience in the cave, Muhammad made his way back home, where he crawled to his wife's side, crying, "Wrap me up! Wrap me up!"

Khadija immediately threw a cloak over him and held him tightly in her arms until the trembling and convulsions stopped. Once he had calmed, Muhammad wept openly as he tried to explain what had happened to him. "Khadija," he said, "I think that I have gone mad."

"This cannot be, my dear," Khadija replied, stroking his hair. "God would not treat you thus since He knows your truthfulness, your great trustworthiness, your fine character, and your kindness."

But because Muhammad remained inconsolable, Khadija gathered her garments about her and sought out the only person she knew who would understand what had happened to her husband: her Christian cousin, Waraqa, the same Waraqa who had been one of the original Hanifs before converting to Christianity. Waraqa was familiar enough with the scriptures to recognize Muhammad's experience for what it was.

"He is a prophet of this people," Waraqa assured his cousin after hearing her story. "Bid him be of good heart."

Still, Muhammad was unsure about what he was supposed to do now that he had been called by God. To make matters worse, when he needed assurance the most, God turned mute. That first revelatory experience on Mount Hira was followed by a long period of silence, so that after a while even Khadija, who never doubted the truth of Muhammad's experience, began to question the meaning of it.

Finally, when Muhammad was at his lowest, a second verse was sent down from heaven in the same painfully violent manner as the first, this one assuring Muhammad that, whether he liked it or not, he was now the Messenger of God:

By the grace of your Lord, you are not a madman.
Yours will be an unending reward;
For you are a man of noble character.
Soon, you shall see, and they shall see, who the madman is.
  (68:1–5)

Now Muhammad no longer had any choice but to accept his calling.

The earliest verses that Muhammad revealed to the Meccans can be divided into two major themes, religious and social—though the same language was employed for both. First, Muhammad sang of the power and glory of the God who "cracked open the earth and caused to grow in it corn and grapes and clover and olives and dates and orchards dense with trees" (80:19). This was not the same powerful and distant High God with whom most people in Mecca were already familiar. This was a *good* God who deeply loved

33

creation. This God was *al-Rahman*, "the most merciful" (55:1), *al-Akram*, "the most generous" (96:3). As such, this was a God worthy of gratitude and worship.

Noticeably absent in these early verses of the Quran about the power and goodness of God is either an authoritative declaration of monotheism or a definitive critique of polytheism. In the beginning, Muhammad seemed more concerned with revealing what kind of god Allah was, not how many gods there were. Perhaps this is because, as previously mentioned, Muhammad was addressing a community that already possessed some measure of monotheistic—or at the very least, henotheistic—tendencies. The Quraysh did not need to be told there was only one god; they'd heard that message many times before from the Jews, the Christians, and the Hanifs, and they did not necessarily disagree. At this point in his ministry, Muhammad had a far more urgent message.

That message—the second theme informing the bulk of Muhammad's earliest recitations—dealt almost exclusively with the demise of the tribal ethic in Mecca. In the strongest terms, Muhammad decried the mistreatment and exploitation of the weak and unprotected. He called for an end to false contracts and the practice of usury that had made slaves of the poor. He spoke of the rights of the underprivileged and the oppressed, and made the astonishing claim that it was the duty of the rich and powerful to take care of them. "Do not oppress the orphan," the Quran commands, "and do not drive away the beggar" (93:9–10).

This was not friendly advice; it was a warning. God had seen the greed and wickedness of the Quraysh and would tolerate it no longer.

Woe to every slanderer and backbiter
Who amasses wealth, hoarding it to himself.
Does he really think his wealth will make him immortal?
By no means! He will be cast into . . .
The fire kindled by God. (104:1–6)

More than anything else, Muhammad considered himself
a warner carrying a message for those in his community who
continued to abuse the orphan, who did not induce others to
feed the needy, who prayed to the gods while remaining oblivi-
ous to their moral duties, and who withheld things of common use from others (107:1–7). His message was simple: The
Day of Judgment was coming, when "the sky will be cleft
asunder and the earth shall be leveled" (84:1–3), and those
who did not "free the slave" or "feed others in times of famine"
would be engulfed in fire (90:13–20).

This was a radical message, one that had never been heard
before in Mecca. Muhammad was not yet establishing a new
religion; he was calling for sweeping social reform. He was
not yet preaching monotheism; he was demanding economic
justice. And for this revolutionary and profoundly innovative
message, he was more or less ignored.

Early Followers

All of the traditions claim that, at first, Muhammad confined
the Revelation to his closest friends and family members. The
first person to accept his message was obviously Khadija, who,
from the moment she met him to the moment she died, remained by her husband, especially during those times when

he was at his lowest. While there is a great deal of sectarian debate among Muslims as to who the second person to accept the message was, it is safe to assume it would have been Muhammad's cousin, Ali, who as Abu Talib's son had grown up in the same household as the Prophet and was the closest person to him after his wife.

Ali's acceptance came as a great relief to Muhammad, for he was not only Muhammad's cousin, he was also his closest ally: the man whom the Prophet repeatedly referred to as "brother." Ali would eventually mature into the most respected warrior in Islam. He would marry Muhammad's beloved daughter, Fatima, and provide the Prophet with his legendary grandsons, Hasan and Husayn. Considered the fount of esoteric knowledge and the father of Islamic metaphysics, Ali would one day inspire an entirely new sect in Islam. However, at the moment when he stood up as the first among the Banu Hashim to respond to the Prophet's call, he was only a thirteen-year-old boy.

Ali's conversion was promptly followed by the conversion of Muhammad's slave, Zayd, whom he naturally freed. Soon afterward, Abu Bakr, Muhammad's dear friend and a wealthy Qurayshi merchant, became a follower. He was a deeply loyal and fervently pious man, whose first act after accepting Muhammad's message was to spend his wealth buying and freeing the slaves of his fellow merchants until he had almost nothing left. Through Abu Bakr, the message was dispersed throughout the city, for as Ibn Hisham testifies, he was not the sort to keep such things to himself but "showed his faith openly and called others to God and his apostle."

There are several remarkable aspects of Muhammad's movement in Mecca. While his message had eventually reached nearly every sector of society—from the weak and unprotected whose rights he advocated, to the Meccan elite whom he preached against—the most surprising feature of his movement during those early years is that its followers consisted primarily of what the scholar Montgomery Watt has called "the most influential families in the most influential clans." These were young men, the majority under thirty years old, who felt the same discontent with Meccan society as Muhammad did. And yet, they were not all men: A great many of Muhammad's earliest followers were women, many of whom risked their lives in rejecting the traditions of their fathers, husbands, and brothers to join his movement.

Regardless, Muhammad's reticence during those first few years kept this a small group of about thirty to forty people who referred to themselves as Muhammad's Companions, for at this point, that was all they were. As far as everyone else in Mecca was concerned, Muhammad's message and his Companions were best ignored.

The Impact of "No god but God"

In 613, three years after the Revelation had begun, Muhammad's message underwent a dramatic transformation, one that is best summed up in the twofold profession of faith, or *shahadah*, that would henceforth define both the mission and principles of the movement: There is no god but God, and Muhammad is God's Messenger.

From this point forward in Muhammad's ministry, the monotheism that had been implicit in the earliest recitations became the dominant theology behind what had thus far been primarily a social message. "Proclaim to them what you have been commanded," God demands, "and turn away from the polytheists" (15:94).

While it is commonly assumed that it was this new, uncompromising monotheism that ultimately brought the wrath of the Quraysh upon Muhammad and his small band of followers, such a view fails to appreciate the profound social and economic consequences implied by this simple statement of faith.

It is important to bear in mind that the Quraysh were quite sophisticated with regard to religion. After all, they made their living off it. Polytheism, henotheism, monotheism, Christianity, Judaism, Zoroastrianism, Hanifism, paganism in all its varieties—the Quraysh had seen it all. It is difficult to believe they would have been shocked by Muhammad's monotheistic claims. Not only had the Hanifs been preaching the same thing for years, but the traditions list a number of other well-known prophetic figures living throughout the Hijaz who also preached monotheism. In fact, the early Muslims revered two of these "prophets"—Suwayd and Luqman—as Muhammad's predecessors. Luqman even has his own chapter in the Quran (31), in which he is called a man upon whom God had bestowed great wisdom. So, theologically speaking, Muhammad's assertion that "there is no god but God" would have been neither scandalous nor, for that matter, original in Mecca.

There are, however, two very important factors that distinguished Muhammad from the rest of his contemporaries, factors that would have enraged the Quraysh far more than his monotheistic beliefs.

First, unlike Luqman and the Hanifs, Muhammad did not

speak from his own authority. On the contrary, what made Muhammad unique was his claim to be the Messenger of God. He even went so far as to identify himself repeatedly with the Jewish and Christian prophets and messengers who had come before him, particularly with Abraham, whom all Meccans—pagan or otherwise—regarded as a divinely inspired prophet. In short, the difference between Muhammad and the Hanifs was that Muhammad was not just preaching "the religion of Abraham," Muhammad was the new Abraham (6:83–86; 21:51–93). And it was precisely this self-image that so greatly disturbed the Quraysh. For by proclaiming himself the Messenger of God, Muhammad was blatantly transgressing the traditional Arab process through which power was granted. This was not authority that had been given to Muhammad as "the first among equals." Muhammad had no equals.

Second, as mentioned, the Hanif preachers may have attacked the polytheism and greed of their fellow Meccans, but they maintained a deep reverence for the Ka'ba and those in the community who acted as Keepers of the Keys. That would explain why the Hanifs appear to have been tolerated in Mecca, and why they never converted in great numbers to Muhammad's movement. But as a businessman and a merchant himself, Muhammad understood what the Hanifs could not: The only way to bring about radical social and economic reform in Mecca was to overturn the religio-economic system on which the city was built; and the only way to do that was to attack the very source of the Quraysh's wealth and prestige—the Ka'ba.

"There is no god but God" was, for Muhammad, far more than a profession of faith. This statement was a conscious and deliberate attack on both the Ka'ba and the sacred right of the Quraysh to manage it. And because the religious and economic lives of Mecca were inextricably linked, any attack on one was necessarily an attack on the other.

Certainly the shahadah contained an important theological innovation, but that innovation was not monotheism. With this simple profession of faith, Muhammad was declaring to Mecca that the God of the heavens and the earth required no intermediaries whatsoever but could be accessed by anyone. Thus, the idols in the sanctuary, and indeed the sanctuary itself, insofar as it served as a repository for the gods, were utterly useless. And if the Ka'ba was useless, then there was no more reason for Mecca's supremacy as either the religious or the economic center of the Hijaz.

This message the Quraysh could not ignore, especially with the pilgrimage season fast approaching. They tried everything to silence Muhammad and his Companions. They went to Abu Talib for help, but the Shaykh of Hashim, though he would never accept Muhammad's message himself, refused to withdraw his protection from his nephew. They poured contempt on Muhammad and abused those of his Companions who did not have the good fortune of being protected by a Shaykh. They even offered Muhammad all the freedom, support, power, and money he wanted to continue his movement in peace, so long as he ceased insulting their forefathers, mocking their customs, dividing their families, and, above all, cursing the other gods in the sanctuary. But Muhammad refused, and as the time came for the pilgrims to gather once again at Mecca with their prayers and their merchandise, the anxiety of the Quraysh reached new heights.

The Quraysh knew that Muhammad intended to stand at

40

the Ka'ba and deliver his message personally to the pilgrims gathering from all over the Peninsula. And while this might not have been the first time a preacher had condemned the Quraysh and their practices, it was certainly the first time such condemnation was coming from a successful and well-known Qurayshi businessman—that is, "one of their own." Recognizing this as a threat that could not be tolerated, the Quraysh embarked on a strategy to preempt Muhammad's plan by sitting "on the paths which men take when they come to the fair" and warning everyone who passed that "a sorcerer, who has brought a message by which he separates a man from his father, or from his brother, or from his wife, or from his family" awaited them at the Ka'ba and should be ignored.

The Quraysh did not really believe that Muhammad was a sorcerer; they freely admitted that his recitations came with "no spitting and no knots," rituals that were apparently associated with sorcery. But they were absolutely earnest in their conviction that Muhammad was dividing the families of Mecca. Conversion to Muhammad's movement meant not only changing one's faith but also cutting oneself off from the activities of the tribe, in essence, removing oneself from the tribe.

This was a serious concern for the Quraysh, whose chief complaint against Muhammad (at least publicly) was neither his call for social and financial reform nor his radical monotheism. Indeed, in the whole of the Quran, there exists not a single Qurayshi defense of polytheism that rests on the conviction of its truth. Rather, as indicated by their warnings to the pilgrims, the Quraysh seemed more disturbed by Muhammad's insistent derision of the rituals and traditional values of their forefathers, traditions upon which the social, religious, and economic foundation of the city rested, than they were by his message of monotheism.

Predictably, however, their warning to ignore "the sorcerer" standing at the Ka'ba only increased interest in Muhammad's message, so that by the time the pilgrimage cycle and the desert fairs were complete and the pilgrims had departed for their homes, Muhammad—the man who had so frightened the untouchable Quraysh—was talked about throughout Arabia.

After failing to silence Muhammad during the pilgrimage fair, the Quraysh decided to take a page from the Prophet's book and attack Muhammad in the same way he had attacked them: economically. A boycott was placed not just on Muhammad and his Companions but, in true tribal fashion, on Muhammad's entire clan. Henceforth, no one in Mecca was allowed to marry into, buy merchandise from, or sell goods (including food and water) to any member of the Banu Hashim, regardless of whether they were followers of Muhammad.

The boycott was not an attempt by the Quraysh to starve the Companions out of Mecca; it was merely a way of demonstrating the consequences of removing oneself from the tribe. If Muhammad and his Companions wished to be separated from the social and religious activities of Mecca, then they must be prepared to be separated from its economy. After all, if religion and trade were inseparable in Mecca, no one could so brazenly deny the former and still expect to participate in the latter.

As intended, the boycott was devastating to the Companions, most of whom, including Muhammad, were still making their living from trade. In fact, the boycott was so destructive that it was protested by prominent members of the Quraysh who had rejected Muhammad but who could no longer bear to "eat food, drink drink, and wear clothes, while the Banu Hashim were perishing." After some months, the boycott was lifted, and the Banu Hashim were once again allowed to join in the commerce of the city. But just as he seemed to be regaining ground in Mecca, tragedy struck Muhammad in the form of the nearly simultaneous deaths of his uncle and protector, Abu Talib, and his wife and confidante, Khadija.

The significance of losing Abu Talib is obvious: Muhammad could no longer rely on his uncle's unwavering protection to keep him from harm. The new Shaykh of Banu Hashim, Abu Lahab, loathed Muhammad personally and made a formal withdrawal of his protection. The results were immediate. Muhammad was openly abused on the streets of Mecca. He could no longer preach or pray in public. When he tried to do so, one person poured dirt over his head, and another threw a sheep's uterus at him.

The loss of Abu Talib may have placed Muhammad in a precarious situation, but the death of Khadija left him absolutely devastated. She was, after all, not only his wife but also his support and comfort, the person who had lifted him out of his poverty, who had quite literally saved his life. In a polygamous society, in which both men and women were allowed an unlimited number of spouses, Muhammad's monogamous relationship with a woman fifteen years his elder was remarkable, to say the least. The loss of Abu Talib's protection was certainly demoralizing, if not detrimental to Muhammad's physical security. But returning home after one of his painfully violent revelatory experiences, or after suffering abuses from the Quraysh, and not having Khadija there to

43

wrap him in her cloak and hold him in her arms until the terror subsided must have been an unimaginable sorrow for the Prophet.

With the loss of both his physical and his emotional support, Muhammad could no longer remain in Mecca. Some time earlier, he had sent a small group of his followers—those without any form of protection in Meccan society—temporarily to Abyssinia, partly to seek asylum from its Christian emperor, partly in an attempt to ally himself with one of the Quraysh's chief commercial rivals. But now Muhammad needed a permanent home where he and his Companions could be free from the unrestrained wrath of the Quraysh.

He tried Mecca's sister city, Ta'if, but its tribal leaders were not inclined to antagonize the Quraysh by giving refuge to their enemy. He visited the local fairs around Mecca, but to no avail. Finally, the answer came in the form of an invitation from a small clan called the *Khazraj*, who lived in an agricultural oasis some two hundred fifty miles north of Mecca—a conglomeration of villages known collectively as *Yathrib*. Although Yathrib was a distant and totally foreign city, Muhammad had no choice but to accept the invitation and prepare his Companions to do the unthinkable: abandon their tribe and their families for an uncertain future in a place where they would be without protection.

The *Hijra*, or emigration to Yathrib, occurred slowly and stealthily, with the Companions heading out toward the oasis a few at a time. By the time the Quraysh realized what was happening, only Muhammad, Abu Bakr, and Ali were left. Fearing that Muhammad was leaving Mecca to raise an army, the various clan Shaykhs decided to choose one man from each family, "a young, powerful, well-born, aristocratic warrior," who would sneak into Muhammad's house while he was asleep and simultaneously drive their swords into his body, thereby placing the responsibility for his death upon everyone in the tribe. Having learned about the attempt on his life the night before, Muhammad and Abu Bakr had slipped out of the house through a window and fled the city.

The Quraysh were furious. They offered a massive bounty of a hundred she-camels to anyone who could find Muhammad and bring him back to Mecca. The unusually high reward attracted dozens of Bedouin tribesmen, who combed the surrounding area night and day looking for the Prophet and his friend.

Meanwhile, Muhammad and Abu Bakr had taken cover in a cave not far from Mecca. For three days and nights they hid from view, waiting for the hunt to subside and the Bedouin to return to their camps. On the third night, they carefully crept out of the cave and, making sure no one was following, mounted two camels brought to them by a sympathetic conspirator. They then quietly disappeared into the desert on their way to Yathrib.

4

Muhammad in Medina

Medina's Significance

There exists an enduring mythology about Muhammad's time in the city that would bear his name, the city where Muhammad's Arab social reform movement would transform into a universal religious ideology. Years later, when Muslim scholars sought to establish a distinctly Islamic calendar, they would begin not with the birth of the Prophet, nor with the onset of Revelation, but with the year Muhammad and his band of followers—now known as the Emigrants—migrated from Mecca to this small federation of villages to start a new society with the help of the *Ansar,* or "Helpers," that handful of Yathrib's villagers who had accepted Muhammad's message and converted to his movement. That year, 622 C.E., would ultimately become known as Year 1 A.H. (After Hijra); and the oasis that for centuries had been called Yathrib would henceforth be celebrated as *Medinat an-Nabi:* "The City of the Prophet," or more simply, Medina.

Muhammad's time in Medina became the paradigm for the Muslim empires that expanded throughout the Middle East after the Prophet's death, and the standard that every Arab kingdom struggled to meet during the Middle Ages. The Medinan ideal inspired the various Islamic revivalist movements of the eighteenth and nineteenth centuries, all of which strove to return to the original values of Muhammad's unadulterated community as a means to wrest control of Muslim lands from colonial rule (though the revivalists had radically different ideas about how to define those original values). And with the demise of colonialism in the twentieth century, it was the memory of Medina that launched the notion of the Islamic state.

Today, Medina is simultaneously the archetype of Islamic democracy and the impetus for Islamic militancy. Islamic modernists point to Muhammad's community in Medina as proof that Islam advocates the separation of religious and temporal power. Muslim extremists use the same community to fashion various models of Muslim theocracy. In their struggle for equal rights, Muslim feminists have consistently drawn inspiration from the legal reforms Muhammad instituted in Medina, while at the same time, Muslim traditionalists have construed those same legal reforms as grounds for maintaining the subjugation of women in Islamic society. For some, Muhammad's actions in Medina serve as the model for Muslim-Jewish relations; for others, they demonstrate the insurmountable conflict that has always existed, and will always exist, between the two sons of Abraham. Yet regardless of whether one is labeled a modernist or a traditionalist, a

47

reformist or a fundamentalist, a feminist or a misogynist, all Muslims regard Medina as the model of Islamic perfection. Put simply, Medina is what Islam was meant to be.

As with all mythologies of this magnitude, it is often difficult to separate fact from myth. Part of the problem is that the historical traditions dealing with Muhammad's time in Medina were written hundreds of years after the Prophet's death, by Muslim historians who were keen to emphasize the universal recognition and immediate success of Muhammad's divine mission. Muhammad's biographers were living at a time in which the Muslim community had already become an enormously powerful empire. As a result, their accounts more often reflect the political and religious ideologies of ninth-century Damascus, or eleventh-century Baghdad, than that of seventh-century Medina.

So, to understand what really happened in Medina and why, one must sift through the sources to uncover the remote desert oasis that nurtured and cultivated the community in its infancy, not the holy city that would become the capital of the Muslim community. After all, long before there was a City of the Prophet, there was only Yathrib.

Historical Medina

Yathrib in the seventh century was a thriving agricultural oasis thick with palm orchards and vast arable fields, most of which were dominated by twenty clans of Jewish Arabs. Apart from their religious designation as Jews, little differentiated them from their pagan neighbors. Like all Arabs, the Jews of Yathrib considered themselves, first and foremost, members of their own individual clans—each of which acted as a sovereign entity—rather than as a single community of Jews. And while a few Jewish clans may have had alliances with one another, even these in no way constituted a united Jewish tribe.

As the earliest settlers in the region, the Jews occupied Yathrib's most fertile agricultural lands, called the Heights, quickly becoming masters of Arabia's most prized crop: dates. They were also skilled jewelers, clothiers, arms makers, and vintners. However, it was Yathrib's dates, coveted throughout the Hijaz, that had made them rich. Five of the largest Jewish clans in the oasis—the Banu Thalabah, the Banu Hadl, the Banu Qurayza, the Banu Nadir, and the Banu Qaynuqa (who also controlled the city's sole market)—enjoyed an almost complete monopoly over Yathrib's economy.

By the time a number of Bedouin tribes gave up their nomadic existence and also settled in Yathrib, all the most fertile lands had already been claimed. What remained were the barely cultivable lots situated in a region termed the Bottom. The competition over limited resources had not only created some conflict between the pagan and Jewish clans, it had also resulted in a gradual decline of the Jews' authority and influence in Yathrib. For the most part, however, the two groups lived in relative peace through strategic tribal affiliations and economic alliances. The Jews regularly employed the Arabs to transport their dates to nearby markets (especially in Mecca), while the Arabs maintained a high esteem for the learning, craftsmanship, and heritage of their Jewish neighbors.

The real conflict in the oasis was not between the Jews and Arabs but among the Arabs themselves, and more specifically between Yathrib's two largest Arab tribes: the *Aws* and the Khazraj. While the origins of this conflict have been lost to history, what seems clear is that the Law of Retribution had failed to solve the long-standing quarrel. By the time Muhammad arrived in Yathrib, what had probably begun as a disagreement over limited resources had escalated into a bloody feud that had spilled over even to the Jewish clans, with the Banu Nadir and the Banu Qurayza supporting the Aws, and the Banu Qaynuqa siding with the Khazraj. In short, this conflict was splitting the oasis in two. What the Aws and the Khazraj desperately needed was a Hakam, an arbiter. Not just any Hakam but an authoritative, trustworthy, and neutral party who was totally unconnected with anyone in Yathrib, someone who had the power to arbitrate between the two tribes. How fortunate, then, that the perfect man for the job was himself in desperate need of a place to live.

The Constitution of Medina

That Muhammad came to Yathrib as little more than the Hakam in the quarrel between the Aws and the Khazraj is certain. Yet the traditions seem to present Muhammad arriving in the oasis as the mighty prophet of a new and firmly established religion, and as the unchallenged leader of the whole of Yathrib. This view is partly the result of a famous document called the Constitution of Medina, which Muhammad may have drafted some time after settling in the oasis. The document was a series of formal agreements of nonaggression among Muhammad, the Emigrants, the Ansar, and the rest of Yathrib's clans, both Jewish and pagan. The Constitution is controversial, however, because it seems to assign to Muhammad unparalleled religious and political authority over the entire population of the oasis, including the Jews. It indicates

50

that Muhammad had sole authority to arbitrate all disputes in Yathrib, not just those between the Aws and Khazraj. It declares him to be Yathrib's sole war leader (Qa'id) and unequivocally recognizes him as the Messenger of God. And while it implies that Muhammad's primary role was as Shaykh of his "clan" of Emigrants, it also clearly endows him with a privileged position over all other tribal and clan Shaykhs in Yathrib.

The problem lies in determining exactly when the Constitution of Medina was written. The traditional sources, including al-Tabari and Ibn Hisham, place its composition among the Prophet's first acts upon entering the oasis: in 622 C.E. But that is highly unlikely, given Muhammad's weak position during those first few years in Yathrib. In fact, it was not until after the Battle of Badr in 624, or perhaps not even until 627, that the majority of the Aws tribe converted to Islam. Before then, few people outside the Ansar (which at that point consisted of only a handful of members from the Khazraj tribe) would have known who Muhammad was, let alone have submitted to his authority. His movement represented the tiniest fraction of Yathrib's population; the Jews alone may have totaled in the thousands. When Muhammad arrived in the oasis, he had brought fewer than a hundred men, women, and children with him.

The Constitution of Medina may reflect several early pacts of nonaggression among Muhammad, the Arab clans, and their Jewish clients. It may even reproduce certain elements of Muhammad's arbitration between the Aws and the Khazraj. But there is simply no way it could have been completed as it has been preserved before 624 C.E.

51

The Ummah

Muhammad's role during those first couple of years in Yathrib was very likely that of a Hakam—albeit a powerful and divinely inspired one—whose arbitration was restricted to the Aws and Khazraj, and whose authority as a Shaykh was confined to his own "clan" of Emigrants: one clan out of many, one Shaykh out of many. Muhammad's claim to be the Messenger of God would not have had to be either accepted or rejected for him to function properly in either of these two roles. Both the pagan Arabs and the Jews of Yathrib would have considered his prophetic consciousness to be proof of his supernatural wisdom, especially since the ideal Hakam was almost always also the Kahin, whose connection to the Divine was indispensable in especially difficult disputes like the one between the Aws and Khazraj.

Yet while the other inhabitants of Yathrib may have viewed Muhammad as little more than a Hakam and a Shaykh, that was not at all how the Emigrants saw him. To his small band of followers, Muhammad was the Prophet/Lawgiver who spoke with the authority of the one God. As such, he had come to Yathrib to establish a new kind of community, though how that community was to be organized, and who could be considered a member of it, had yet to be defined. It may be tempting to call the members of this new community *Muslims* (literally, "those who submit" to God), but there is no reason to believe that this term was used to designate a distinct religious movement until many years later. It is more accurate to refer to Muhammad's followers by the same term the Quran uses: the *Ummah*. The problem with the term *Ummah* is that no one is certain what it meant or where it came from.

It may be derived from Arabic, Hebrew, or Aramaic; it may have meant "a community," "a nation," or "a people." A few scholars have suggested that *Ummah* may be derived from the Arabic word for "mother" (*umm*), and while this idea may be aesthetically pleasing, there is no linguistic evidence for it. To make matters more complicated, the word *Ummah* inexplicably ceases to be used in the Quran after 625 C.E., when it is replaced with the word *qawm*—Arabic for "tribe."

Despite its unique nature, the Ummah (the word meaning "community") acted just like any other tribe. After all, Muhammad's community was still an Arab institution based on Arab notions of tribal society. There was simply no alternative model of social organization in seventh-century Arabia, save monarchy. Indeed, there are so many parallels between the early Muslim community and traditional tribal societies that one is left with the distinct impression that, at least in Muhammad's mind, the Ummah was a tribe, though a new and radically innovative one.

For one thing, the reference in the Constitution of Medina to Muhammad's role as Shaykh of his clan of Emigrants indicates that despite the Prophet's elevated status, his secular authority would have fallen well within the traditional paradigm of pre-Islamic tribal society. What is more, just as membership in the tribe obliged participation in the rituals and activities of the tribal cult, so did membership in Muhammad's community require ritual involvement in what could be termed its "tribal cult": in this case, the nascent religion of Islam.

Public rituals like communal prayer, almsgiving, and collective fasting—the first three activities mandated by God—when combined with shared dietary regulations and purity requirements, functioned in the Ummah in much the same way that the activities of the tribal cult did in pagan societies: by providing a common social and religious identity that allowed one group to distinguish itself from another.

What made the Ummah a unique experiment in social organization was that, in Yathrib, far away from the social and religious hegemony of the Quraysh, Muhammad finally had the opportunity to implement the reforms he had been preaching to no avail in Mecca. By enacting a series of radical religious, social, and economic reforms, he was able to establish a new kind of society, the likes of which had never before been seen in Arabia.

For instance, whereas power in the tribe was allocated to a number of figures, none of whom had any real executive authority, Muhammad instead united all the pre-Islamic positions of authority unto himself. He was not only the Shaykh of his community but also its Hakam, its Qa'id, and, as the only legitimate connection to the Divine, its Kahin. His authority as Prophet/Lawgiver was absolute. Also, while the only way to become a member of a tribe was to be born into it, anyone could join Muhammad's community simply by declaring, "There is no god but God, and Muhammad is God's Messenger." The shahadah was thus transformed in Yathrib from a theological statement with explicit social and political implications into a new version of the oath of allegiance, the *bay'ah,* which the tribe gave to its Shaykh. And because neither ethnicity nor culture nor race nor kinship had any significance to Muhammad, the Ummah, unlike a traditional tribe, had an almost unlimited capacity for growth through conversion.

As was the case with all tribal Shaykhs, Muhammad's

primary function as head of the Ummah was to ensure the protection of every member in his community. This he did through the chief means at his disposal: the Law of Retribution. But while retribution was maintained as a legitimate response to injury, Muhammad urged believers toward forgiveness: "The retribution for an injury is an equal injury," the Quran states, "but those who forgive the injury and make reconciliation will be rewarded by God" (42:40). Likewise, the Constitution of Medina sanctions retribution as the principal deterrent for crime, but with the unprecedented stipulation that the entire community may be "solidly against [the criminal], and may do nothing except oppose him," a stark reversal of tribal tradition and a clear indication that Muhammad was already beginning to lay the foundations of a society built on moral rather than utilitarian principles. But this was only the beginning.

To further his egalitarian ideals, Muhammad equalized the blood-worth of every member of his community, so that no longer could one life be considered more or less valuable (monetarily speaking) than another. This was yet another innovation in the Arabian legal system, for while an injury to a victim's eye in pre-Islamic Arabia would have required an equal injury to the criminal's eye, no one would have considered a Shaykh's eye to be worth the same amount as an orphan's. But Muhammad changed all that, and not without seriously disrupting the social order.

Muhammad's move toward egalitarianism did not end with reforming the Law of Retribution. In Yathrib, he categorically outlawed usury (the charging of interest), the abuse of which was one of his chief complaints against the Meccan religio-economic system. To facilitate the new economy, he established his own market, which, unlike the one controlled by the Banu Qaynuqa, charged no tax on transactions and no interest on loans. While this tax-free market eventually became a point of conflict between Muhammad and the Banu Qaynuqa, the Prophet's move was not a means of antagonizing the Qaynuqa but a further step toward alleviating the divide between the ridiculously wealthy and the absurdly poor.

Using his unquestioned religious authority, Muhammad instituted a mandatory tithe called *zakat,* which every member of the Ummah had to pay according to his or her means. Once collected, the money was then redistributed as alms to the community's neediest members. *Zakat* literally means "purification," and was not an act of charity but of religious devotion: Benevolence and care for the poor were the first and most enduring virtues preached by Muhammad in Mecca. The Quran reminds believers that piety lies "not in turning your face East or West in prayer . . . but in distributing your wealth out of love for God to your needy kin; to the orphans, to the vagrants, and to the mendicants; it lies in freeing the slaves, in observing your devotions, and in giving alms to the poor" (2:177).

There was even more change to come in Medina. Muhammad—who had benefited greatly from the wealth and stability provided by Khadija—strove to give women the opportunity to attain some level of equality and independence in society by amending Arabia's traditional marriage and inheritance laws to remove the obstacles that prohibited women from inheriting and maintaining their own wealth (in a single revolutionary move, he both limited how many wives a man could marry and granted women the right to divorce their husbands). While the exact changes Muhammad made to this tradition are far too complex to discuss in detail here, it is sufficient to note that women in the Ummah were, for the first time, given the right both to inherit the property of their husbands and to keep their dowries as their own personal property throughout the marriage. Muhammad also forbade a husband to touch his wife's dowry, forcing him instead to provide for his family from his own wealth. If the husband died, his wife would inherit a portion of his property; if he divorced her, the entire dowry was hers to take back to her family.

As one would expect, Muhammad's innovations did not sit well with the male members of his community. If women could no longer be considered property, men complained, not only would men's wealth be drastically reduced, but their own meager inheritances would now have to be split with their sisters and daughters—members of the community who, they argued, did not share an equal burden with the men. Al-Tabari recounts how some of these men brought their grievances to Muhammad, asking, "How can one give the right of inheritance to women and children, who do not work and do not earn their living? Are they now going to inherit just like men who have worked to earn that money?"

Muhammad's response to these complaints was both unsympathetic and shockingly unyielding. "Those who disobey God and His Messenger, and who try to overstep the boundaries of this [inheritance] law, will be thrown into Hell, where they will dwell forever, suffering the most shameful punishment" (4:14).

Muhammad's Wives

After having lived a monogamous life with Khadija for more than twenty-five years, Muhammad, in the course of ten years in Yathrib, married nine different women. However, with very few exceptions, these marriages were not sexual unions but political ones. This is not to say that Muhammad was uninterested in sex; on the contrary, the traditions present him as a man with a robust and healthy libido. But as Shaykh of the Ummah, it was Muhammad's responsibility to forge links within and beyond his community through the only means at his disposal: marriage. Thus, his unions with Aisha and Hafsah linked him to the two most important and influential leaders of the early Muslim community—to Abu Bakr and Umar, respectively. His marriage to Umm Salamah a year later forged an important relationship with one of Mecca's most powerful clans, the Makhzum. His union with Sawdah— by all accounts an unattractive widow long past the age of marriage—served as an example to the Ummah to marry those women in need of financial support. His marriage to Rayhana, a Jew, linked him with the Banu Qurayza, while his marriage to Mariyah, a Christian and a Copt, created a significant political alliance with the ruler of Egypt.

Nevertheless, for fourteen hundred years—from the medieval Popes of the Crusades to the Enlightenment philosophers of Europe to evangelical preachers in the United States—Muhammad's wives have been the source of numerous lurid attacks against the Prophet and the religion of Islam. In response, contemporary scholars—Muslim and non-Muslim alike—have done considerable work to defend Muhammad's marriages, especially his union with Aisha, who was nine years old when betrothed to the Prophet. While these scholars should be commended for their work in debunking the bigoted and ignorant critiques of anti-Islamic preachers and pundits, the fact is that Muhammad needs no defense on this point.

Like the great Jewish patriarchs Abraham and Jacob; like the prophets Moses and Hosea; like the Israelite kings Saul, David, and Solomon; and like nearly all of the Christian/ Byzantine and Zoroastrian/Sasanian monarchs, all Shaykhs in Arabia—Muhammad included—had either multiple wives, multiple concubines, or both. In seventh-century Arabia, a Shaykh's power and authority was in large part determined by the size of his harem. And while Muhammad's union with a nine-year-old girl may be shocking to our modern sensibilities, his betrothal to Aisha was just that: a betrothal. Aisha did not consummate her marriage to Muhammad until after reaching puberty, which is when every girl in Arabia without exception became eligible for marriage. The most shocking aspect of Muhammad's marriages is not his ten years of polygamy in Yathrib but his twenty-five years of monogamy in Mecca, something practically unheard of at the time. Indeed, if there is anything at all interesting or unusual about Muhammad's marriages, it is not how many wives he had but rather the regulations that were imposed on them, specifically with regard to the veil.

Although long seen as the most distinctive emblem of Islam, the veil is, surprisingly, not specifically enjoined upon Muslim women anywhere in the Quran. The tradition of veiling and seclusion (known together as *hijab*) was introduced into Arabia long before Muhammad, primarily through Arab contacts with Syria and Iran, where the hijab was a sign of social status. After all, only a woman who need not work in the fields could afford to remain secluded and veiled.

In the Ummah, there was no tradition of veiling until around 627 c.e., when the so-called "verse of hijab" suddenly descended upon the community. That verse, however, was addressed not to women in general but exclusively to Muhammad's wives: "Believers, do not enter the Prophet's house . . . unless asked. And if you are invited . . . do not linger. And when you ask something from the Prophet's wives, do so from behind a hijab. This will assure the purity of your hearts as well as theirs" (33:53).

This restriction makes perfect sense when one recalls that Muhammad's house was also the community's mosque: the center of religious and social life in the Ummah. People were constantly coming in and out of this compound at all hours. When delegations from other tribes came to speak with Muhammad, they would set up their tents for days at a time inside the open courtyard, just a few feet away from the apartments in which Muhammad's wives slept. And new emigrants who arrived in Yathrib would often stay within the mosque's walls until they could find suitable homes.

When Muhammad was little more than a tribal Shaykh, this constant commotion could be tolerated. But by the year 627, when he had become the supremely powerful leader of an increasingly expanding community, some kind of segregation had to be enforced to maintain the inviolability of his wives. Thus the tradition, borrowed from the upper classes of Iranian and Syrian women, of veiling and secluding the most important women in society from the peering eyes of everyone else.

That the veil applied solely to Muhammad's wives is

further demonstrated by the fact that the term for donning the veil, *darabat al-hijab,* was used synonymously and interchangeably with "becoming Muhammad's wife." For this reason, during the Prophet's lifetime, no other women in the Ummah observed hijab. Of course, modesty was enjoined on all believers, and women in particular were instructed to "draw their clothes around them a little to be recognized as believers and so that no harm will come to them" (33:60). More specifically, women should "guard their private parts . . . and drape a cover (the word here is *khamr,* not *hijab*) over their breasts" when in the presence of strange men (24:31–32). But nowhere in the whole of the Quran is the term *hijab* applied to any woman other than the wives of Muhammad.

It is difficult to say with certainty when the veil was adopted by the rest of the Ummah, though it was most likely long after Muhammad's death. Muslim women probably began wearing the veil as a way to emulate the Prophet's wives, who were revered as "the Mothers of the Ummah." But the veil was neither compulsory nor, for that matter, widely adopted until generations after Muhammad's death, when a large body of male scriptural and legal scholars began using their religious and political authority to regain the dominance they had lost in society as a result of the Prophet's egalitarian reforms.

Muhammad's revolutionary experiment in Medina proved so popular that from 622 to 624 c.e., the Ummah multiplied rapidly, both from the addition of new Ansar and from the influx of new Emigrants eager to join in what was taking place in the City of the Prophet. Though, in truth, this was still only Yathrib. It could not properly be called Medina until after Muhammad turned his attention away from his egalitarian

61

reforms and back toward the sacred city of Mecca and the powerful tribe that held the Hijaz in its grip.

Muhammad and War

At first, the Quraysh seemed to be completely untroubled by the success of Muhammad's community in Yathrib. Certainly they were aware of what was taking place there. The Quraysh preserved their dominant position in Arabia by maintaining spies throughout the Peninsula; nothing that could endanger their authority or threaten their profits would have passed their notice. But while they may have been concerned with the growing number of his followers, as long as they remained confined to Yathrib, Mecca was content to forget all about Muhammad. Muhammad, however, was not willing to forget about Mecca.

Perhaps the greatest transformation that occurred in Yathrib was not in the traditional tribal system but in the Prophet himself. As the Revelation evolved from general statements about the goodness and power of God to specific legal and civil rules for constructing and maintaining a righteous and egalitarian society, so too did Muhammad's prophetic consciousness evolve. No longer was his message to be addressed solely to "the mother of cities [Mecca] and those who dwell around it" (6:92). The dramatic success of the Ummah in Yathrib had convinced Muhammad that God was calling him to be more than just a warner to his "tribe and close kin" (26:214). He now understood his role as being "a mercy to all the creatures of the world" (21:107) and the Messenger "to all of humanity" (12:104; 81:27).

Of course, no matter how popular or successful or large his

community became, it could never hope to expand beyond the borders of Yathrib if the religious, economic, and social center of the Hijaz continued to oppose it. Muhammad would have to confront and, if possible, convert the Quraysh to his side. But first, he had to get their attention.

Having learned in Mecca that the only effective way to confront the Quraysh was through their pocketbooks, Muhammad made the extraordinarily bold decision of declaring Yathrib to be a sanctuary city (*haram*). This declaration, formalized in the Constitution of Medina, meant that Yathrib could now conceivably become both a religious pilgrimage site and a legitimate trading center (the two being almost inseparable in ancient Arabia). This was not merely a financial decision. By declaring Yathrib a sanctuary city, Muhammad was deliberately challenging Mecca's religious and economic hegemony over the Peninsula. And just to make sure the Quraysh got the message, he sent his followers out into the desert to take part in the time-honored Arab tradition of caravan raiding.

In pre-Islamic Arabia, caravan raiding was a legitimate means for small clans to benefit from the wealth of larger ones. It was in no way considered stealing, and as long as no violence occurred and no blood was shed, there was no need for retribution. The raiding party would quickly descend on a caravan—usually at its rear—and carry off whatever they could get their hands on before being discovered. These periodic raids were certainly a nuisance for the caravan leaders, but in general they were considered part of the innate hazards of transporting large amounts of goods through a vast and unprotected desert.

Though small and sporadic at first, Muhammad's raids

not only provided the Ummah with desperately needed income, they also effectively disrupted the trade flowing in and out of Mecca. It wasn't long before caravans entering the sacred city began complaining to the Quraysh that they no longer felt safe traveling through the region.

A few caravans even chose to detour to Yathrib instead to take advantage of the security Muhammad and his men were assuring. Trade began to dwindle in Mecca, profits were lost, and Muhammad finally got the attention he was seeking.

In 624, Muhammad received news that a large caravan was making its way to Mecca from Palestine, the sheer size of which made it too tempting to ignore. Summoning a band of three hundred volunteers, mostly Emigrants, he set out to raid it. But as his group arrived outside the city of Badr, they were suddenly confronted by a thousand Qurayshi warriors. Muhammad's plans had been leaked to Mecca, and now the Quraysh were ready to give his small band of insurgents a lesson they would not forget.

For days the two armies surveyed each other from opposite sides of a sizable valley: the Quraysh arrayed in white tunics, straddling ornately painted horses and tall, brawny camels; the Ummah dressed in rags and prepared for a raid, not a war. In truth, neither side seemed eager for a fight. The Quraysh probably assumed their overwhelming numbers would elicit immediate surrender or, at the very least, contrition. And Muhammad, who must have known that fighting the Quraysh under these circumstances would result not only in his own death but in the end of the Ummah, was anxiously awaiting instructions from God. "O God," he kept praying, "if this band of people perishes, you will no longer be worshipped."

There was something more to Muhammad's reluctance at Badr than fear of annihilation. Although he had known for some time that his message could not expand outside Arabia without the capitulation of the Quraysh, and while he must have recognized that such capitulation would not come without a fight, Muhammad understood that just as the Revelation had forever transformed the socioeconomic landscape of pre-Islamic Arabia, so must it alter the methods and morals of pre-Islamic warfare.

It is not that Arabia was short on "rules of war." A host of regulations existed among the pagan tribes with regard to when and where fighting could take place. But, for the most part, these rules were meant to contain and limit fighting to ensure the tribe's survival, not to establish a code of conduct in warfare. In the same way that absolute morality did not play a significant role in tribal concepts of law and order, neither did it play a role in tribal notions of war and peace.

The doctrine of *jihad*, as it slowly developed in the Quran, was specifically meant to differentiate between pre-Islamic and Islamic notions of warfare, and to infuse the latter with an "ideological/ethical" dimension that, until that point, did not exist in the Arabian Peninsula. At the heart of the doctrine of jihad was the heretofore unrecognized distinction between combatant and noncombatant. Thus, the killing of women, children, monks, rabbis, the elderly, or any other noncombatant was absolutely forbidden under any circumstances. Muslim law eventually expanded on these prohibitions to outlaw the torture of prisoners of war; the mutilation of the dead; rape, molestation, or any kind of sexual violence during combat; the killing of diplomats; the wanton destruction of property; and the demolition of religious or medical institutions—regulations that would one day be incorporated into modern international laws of war.

Perhaps the most important innovation in the doctrine of jihad was its outright prohibition of all but strictly defensive wars. "Fight in the way of God those who fight you," the Quran says, "but do not begin hostilities; God does not like the aggressor" (2:190). Elsewhere, the Quran is more explicit: "Permission to fight is given *only to those who have been oppressed* . . . who have been driven from their homes for saying, 'God is our Lord'" (22:39; emphasis added).

Badr became the first opportunity for Muhammad to put this theory of jihad into practice. According to tradition, as the days passed and the two armies steadily inched closer to each other, Muhammad refused to fight until attacked. Even as the fighting began—in traditional Arab fashion, with hand-to-hand combat between two or three individuals from both sides, at the end of which the field was cleared of corpses, and another set of individuals were chosen to fight—Muhammad remained on his knees, waiting for a message from God. It was Abu Bakr who, having had enough of the Prophet's indecisiveness, finally urged him to rise and take part in the battle that, despite Muhammad's reluctance, had already begun.

"O Prophet of God," Abu Bakr said, "do not call upon your Lord so much; for God will assuredly fulfill what he has promised you."

Muhammad agreed. Rising to his feet, he finally called upon his small band of followers to trust in God and advance in full against the enemy.

What followed was a fierce skirmish. When the fighting stopped and the battlefield was cleared of bodies, there was little doubt as to who had won. Astonishingly, Muhammad had lost only a dozen men, while the Quraysh were thoroughly routed. News of the Prophet's victory over the largest and most powerful tribe in Arabia reached Yathrib long before the victors did. The Ummah was ecstatic. The Battle of Badr proved that God had blessed the Messenger. There were rumors that angels had descended onto the battlefield to slay Muhammad's enemies. After Badr, Muhammad was no longer a mere Shaykh or a Hakam; he and his followers were now the new political power in the Hijaz. And Yathrib was no longer just an agricultural oasis but the seat of that power: the City of the Prophet. Medina.

Over the next few years, there were many more battles fought between Muhammad's community and the Quraysh. Then, in 628 C.E., Muhammad unexpectedly announced that he was going to Mecca to perform the pilgrimage rites at the Ka'ba. Considering that he was in the middle of a bloody and protracted war with the Meccans, this was an absurd decision. He could not have thought the Quraysh, who had spent the past six years trying to kill him, would simply move out of the way while he and his followers circled the sanctuary. But Muhammad remained undaunted. With more than a thousand of his followers marching behind him, he crossed the desert on his way to the city of his birth, shouting fearlessly along the way the pilgrim's chant: "Here I am, O Allah! Here I am!"

The sound of Muhammad and his followers, unarmed and dressed in pilgrims' clothes, loudly proclaiming their presence to their enemies, must have rung like a death knell in Mecca. Surely the end was near if this man could be so audacious as to think he could walk into the sacred city unmolested. The Quraysh, who rushed out to halt Muhammad before he could enter Mecca, were confounded. Meeting him just outside the city, in a place called *Hudaybiyyah,* they made one last attempt to preserve their control of Mecca by offering the Prophet a cease-fire, the conditions of which were so against Muhammad's interests that it must have appeared to the Muslims to be a joke.

The Treaty of Hudaybiyyah proposed that in return for his immediate withdrawal and the unconditional cessation of all caravan raids in the vicinity of Mecca, Muhammad would be allowed to return in the following pilgrimage season, when the sanctuary would be evacuated for a brief time so that he and his followers could perform the pilgrimage rites undisturbed. Adding insult to injury, Muhammad would be required to sign the treaty not as the Apostle of God but only as the tribal head of his community. Given Muhammad's rapidly growing position in the Hijaz, the treaty was preposterous; more than anything, it demonstrated the certainty of Mecca's impending defeat. Perhaps that is why Muhammad's followers, who sensed victory lingering only a few kilometers in front of them, were so incensed when the Prophet actually accepted the terms.

It is difficult to say why Muhammad accepted the Treaty of Hudaybiyyah. He may have been hoping to regroup and wait for an opportune time to return and conquer Mecca by force. He may have been observing the Quranic mandate and jihadi doctrine to "fight until oppression ends and God's law prevails. But if [the enemy] desists, then you must also cease hostilities" (2:193). Whatever the case, the decision to accept the cease-fire and return the following year turned out to be the most decisive moment in the battle between Mecca and

Medina. When ordinary Meccans saw the respect and devotion with which their supposed enemy and his band of "religious zealots" entered their city and circled the Ka'ba, there seemed little incentive to continue supporting the war. A year after that pilgrimage, in 630 C.E., after Muhammad interpreted a skirmish between the Quraysh and some of his followers as a breach of the cease-fire, he marched once more toward Mecca, this time with ten thousand men behind him, only to find the city's inhabitants welcoming him with open arms.

After accepting Mecca's surrender, Muhammad declared a general amnesty for most of his enemies, including those he had fought in battle. Despite the fact that tribal law now made the Quraysh his slaves, Muhammad declared all of Mecca's inhabitants to be free. Only six men and four women were put to death for various crimes, and no one was forced to convert, though everyone had to take an oath of allegiance never again to wage war against the Prophet.

When this business was complete, the Prophet made his way to the Ka'ba. With the help of his cousin and son-in-law, Ali, he lifted the heavy veil covering the sanctuary door and entered the sacred interior. One by one, he carried the idols out before the assembled crowd and, raising them over his head, smashed them to the ground. The various depictions of gods and prophets were all washed away with Zamzam water; all, that is, except the one of Jesus and his mother, Mary. This image the Prophet put his hands over reverently, saying, "Wash out all except what is beneath my hands."

Finally, Muhammad brought out the idol representing the great Syrian god, Hubal, the master of the Ka'ba. As the

Meccans watched, the Prophet unsheathed his sword and hacked the idol into pieces, forever ending the worship of pagan deities at Mecca. The remains of Hubal's statue Muhammad used as a doorstep leading up to the new, sanctified Ka'ba, the sanctuary that would henceforth be known as the House of God, the seat of a wholly new and universal faith: Islam.

5

After Muhammad

The End of the Beginning

The year is 632 C.E., two years after Muhammad walked triumphantly into Mecca and cleansed the Ka'ba in the name of the one God. At that time, he was a robust man at the peak of his political and spiritual power, unquestionably the most dominant leader in Arabia. Ironically, the movement that had begun as an attempt to reclaim the tribal ethic of Arabia's nomadic past had, in many ways, struck the final dagger into the traditional tribal system. Soon there will be only the Muslim community, the enemies of the Muslim community, the client tribes of the Muslim community, and the *dhimmi*, Christians, Jews, and other non-Muslims protected by the Muslim community. Yet despite the enormous power that accompanied his defeat of the Quraysh, Muhammad refused to replace the Meccan aristocracy with a Muslim monarchy; he would be the Keeper of the Keys, but he would not be the King of Mecca. Thus, once the administrative affairs had been settled and delegations—both military and diplomatic—dispatched to inform the rest of the Arab tribes of the new political order in the Hijaz, Muhammad did something completely unexpected: He went back home to Medina.

Muhammad's return to Medina was meant to acknowledge the Ansar, who had provided him with refuge and protection when no one else would. But it was also a statement to the entire community that while Mecca was now the heart of Islam, Medina would forever be its soul. It is in Medina that deputations will gather from all over the Arabian Peninsula with their pledge that "there is no god but God"; it is in Medina that the pillars of the Muslim faith and the foundations of Muslim government will be constructed and debated.

And it is in Medina that the Prophet breathed his last.

Muhammad Dies—632 c.e.

As one can imagine, Muhammad's death in 632, after a lengthy illness, caused great anxiety among his followers, mostly because he had done so little to prepare them for it. He had made no formal statement about who should replace him as leader of the Ummah, or even what kind of leader that person should be. Perhaps he was awaiting a Revelation that never came; perhaps he wanted the Ummah to decide for themselves who should succeed him. Or perhaps, as some were whispering, the Prophet had appointed a successor, someone whose rightful place at the head of the community was being obscured by the internecine power struggles already beginning to take place among the Muslim leadership.

Meanwhile, the Muslim community was growing and expanding faster than anyone could have imagined and was in serious danger of becoming unmanageable. Muhammad's death had only complicated matters, so that some client tribes were now openly rebelling against Muslim control and refusing to pay the zakat (tithe tax) to Medina. As far as these tribes were concerned, Muhammad's death, like the death of any Shaykh, had annulled their oath of allegiance and severed their responsibility to the Ummah.

Even more disconcerting, Muhammad's vision of a divinely inspired state was proving so popular that, throughout the Arabian Peninsula, other regions had begun to replicate it, using their own indigenous leadership and their own native ideology. In Yemen, a man named al-Aswad, who claimed to receive divine messages from a god he called Rahman (an epithet for Allah), had set up his own state independent of Mecca and Medina. In eastern Arabia, another man, Maslama (or Musaylama), had so successfully imitated Muhammad's formula that he had already gathered thousands of followers in Yamama, which he had declared to be a sanctuary city. To modern scholars, the sudden upsurge of these "false prophets" is an indication that Muhammad's movement had filled a definite social and religious vacuum in Arabia. But to the Muslims of the time, they signaled a grave threat to the religious legitimacy and political stability of the Ummah.

Yet the greatest challenge facing the Muslim community after Muhammad's death was neither rebellious tribes nor false prophets but rather the question of how to build a cohesive religious system out of the Prophet's words and deeds, the majority of which existed solely in the memories of the Companions. Islam was still in the process of defining itself

73

when Muhammad died. By 632, the Quran had been neither written down nor collected, let alone canonized. The religious ideals that would become the foundation of Islamic theology existed only in the most rudimentary form. The questions of proper ritual activity or correct legal and moral behavior were, at this point, barely regulated. They did not have to be: Whatever questions one had—whatever issue was raised either through internal conflict or as a result of foreign contact—any confusion whatsoever could simply be brought before the Prophet for a solution. But without Muhammad around to elucidate the will of God, the Ummah was left with the nearly impossible task of figuring out what the Prophet would have said about an issue or a problem.

Obviously, the first and most urgent concern was to choose someone to lead the Ummah in Muhammad's stead, someone who could maintain the community's stability and integrity in the face of its many internal and external challenges. Unfortunately, there was little consensus as to who that leader should be. Some members of the Ansar tried to offer a compromise by choosing co-leaders, one from Mecca and one from Medina, but that was unacceptable to the Quraysh.

It quickly became clear that the only way to maintain both a sense of unity and some measure of historical continuity in the Ummah was to choose a member of the Quraysh to succeed Muhammad, specifically one of the Companions who had made the original Hijra to Medina in 622 (the *Muhajirun*). Muhammad's clan, the Banu Hashim—now dubbed the *ahl al-bayt,* or the "People of the House [of the Prophet]"—agreed that only a member of the Quraysh could lead the Ummah, though they believed the Prophet would have wanted one of them to succeed him. Indeed, quite a large number of Muslims were convinced that during his final pilgrimage to Mecca, Muhammad had publicly designated his cousin and son-in-law, Ali (who had married Muhammad's beloved daughter Fatima), to be his successor. According to traditions, on his way back to Medina, Muhammad had stopped at an oasis called Ghadir al-Khumm and declared, "Whoever has me as his patron, has Ali as his patron (*mawla*)." Yet there were perhaps an equal number of Muslims who not only denied the events at Ghadir al-Khumm but who also vehemently rejected the privileged status of the Banu Hashim as the family of Muhammad.

Successor to the Messenger

To settle matters once and for all, Abu Bakr, Umar, and a prominent Companion named Abu Ubayda met with a group of Ansar leaders for a traditional *shura,* or tribal consultation. And while an enormous amount of ink has been spilled over this historic meeting, it is still not clear exactly who was present or what took place. The only thing about which scholars can be certain is that at its conclusion, Abu Bakr, spurred on by Umar and Abu Ubayda, was selected to be the next leader of the Muslim community and given the apt but rather vague title *Khalifat Rasul Allah,* "the Successor to the Messenger of God"—*Caliph* in English.

What made Abu Bakr's title so appropriate was that nobody was sure what it was supposed to mean. The Quran refers to both Adam and David as God's Caliphs (2:30; 38:26), meaning they served as God's "trustees" or "viceregents" on earth, but this does not seem to be how Abu Bakr was viewed. The evidence suggests that the Caliphate was not meant to be a position of great religious influence. Certainly, the Caliph would be responsible for upholding the institutions of the Muslim faith, but he would not play a significant role in defining religious practice. In other words, Abu Bakr would replace the Prophet as leader of the Ummah, but he would have no prophetic authority. Muhammad was dead; his status as Messenger died with him.

The deliberate ambiguity of his title was a great advantage for Abu Bakr and his immediate successors because it gave them the opportunity to define the position for themselves, something they would do in widely divergent ways. As far as Abu Bakr was concerned, the Caliphate was a *secular* position that closely resembled that of the traditional tribal Shaykh—"the first among equals"—though with the added responsibility of being the community's war leader (Qa'id) and chief judge, both of which were positions inherited from Muhammad.

Abu Bakr was, in many ways, the perfect choice to succeed Muhammad. Nicknamed *al-Siddiq*, "the faithful one," he was a deeply pious and respected man, one of the first converts to Islam and Muhammad's dearest friend. The fact that he had taken over the Friday prayers during Muhammad's lengthy illness was, in the minds of many, proof that the Prophet would have blessed his succession.

As Caliph, Abu Bakr united the community under a single banner and initiated a time of military triumph and reputed social concord that would become known in the Muslim world as the Golden Era of Islam. It was Abu Bakr and his immediate successors—the first four Caliphs, collectively referred to as the *Rashidun,* the "Rightly Guided Ones"—who tended the seed Muhammad had planted in the Hijaz until it sprouted into a dominant and far-reaching empire. While the Ummah expanded into North Africa, the Indian subcontinent, and large swaths of Europe, the Rightly Guided Ones strove to keep the community rooted in the principles of Muhammad—the struggle for justice, the equality of all believers, care for the poor and marginalized—yet civil strife and the incessant power struggles of the early Companions ultimately split the community into competing factions and turned the Caliphate into that form of government most reviled by the ancient Arabs: absolute monarchy.

As with most sacred histories, however, the truth about the era of the Rightly Guided Ones is far more complicated than the traditions suggest. Indeed, the so-called Golden Era of Islam was anything but a time of religious concord and political harmony. From the moment Muhammad died, there arose dozens of conflicting ideas about everything from how to interpret the Prophet's words and deeds to who should do the interpreting, from whom to choose as leader of the community to how the community should be led. It was even unclear who could and could not be considered a member of the Ummah, or, for that matter, what one had to do to be saved.

As is the case with all great religions, it was precisely the arguments, the discord, and the sometimes bloody conflicts that resulted from trying to discern God's will in the absence of God's prophet that gave birth to the varied and wonderfully diverse institutions of the Muslim faith. Of course, early Islam was not nearly as doctrinally divided as early Christianity. But it is nevertheless important to recognize both the political and the religious divisions within the early Muslim community that were so instrumental in defining and developing the faith.

To begin with, the selection of Abu Bakr as Caliph was by no means unanimous. By all accounts, only a handful of the most prominent Companions were present at the shura. The only other serious contender for the leadership of the Muslim community had not even been informed of the meeting until it was over. At the same time that Abu Bakr was accepting the oath of allegiance, or *bay'ah,* Ali was washing the Prophet's body, preparing him for burial. The Banu Hashim fumed, claiming that without Ali, the shura was not representative of the entire Ummah. Likewise, the Ansar, who considered both Ali and Muhammad to be as much Medinan as Meccan—in other words, "one of their own"—complained bitterly about Ali's exclusion. Both groups publicly refused to swear allegiance to the new Caliph.

In truth, Ali was excluded from the shura because of a growing fear among the larger and wealthier clans of the Quraysh that allowing both prophethood and the Caliphate to rest in the hands of a single clan—especially the insignificant Hashim—would too greatly alter the balance of power in the Ummah. Furthermore, there seemed to be some anxiety among certain members of the community, most notably Abu Bakr and Umar, that maintaining a prolonged hereditary leadership within the family of Muhammad would blur the distinction between the *religious* authority of the Prophet and the *secular* authority of the Caliph.

Whatever the justifications, Ali's proponents would not be silenced; so it was left to Umar to silence them himself. Having already beaten the leader of the Ansar, Sa'd ibn Ubayda, into submission, Umar went to the house of Fatima, Ali's wife and Muhammad's daughter, and threatened to burn it down unless she and the rest of the Banu Hashim accepted the will of the shura. Fortunately, Abu Bakr restrained him at the last moment, but the message was clear: The Ummah was too unstable, and the political situation in the Hijaz too volatile, for this kind of open dissent to be tolerated. Ali agreed. For the sake of the community, he and his entire family surrendered their claim to leadership and solemnly swore allegiance to Abu Bakr, though it took another six months of cajoling for them to do so.

As turbulent as the succession to Muhammad may have been, there is one detail that should not be lost in the tumult and confusion that led to Abu Bakr's Caliphate. Implicit in the conflict over who should lead the Ummah was the unanimous conviction among all Muslims that some kind of popular sanction was required to approve the candidate. Certainly, this was not a democratic process; Abu Bakr was appointed through the consultation of a select group of elders, not elected by the Ummah. But the great effort that the Companions went through to achieve some semblance of unanimity is proof that Abu Bakr's appointment would have been meaningless without the consensus of the entire community.

From our privileged position, the succession to Muhammad may seem a chaotic affair full of intimidation and disorder: a rigged process, to say the least. But it was a process, nonetheless; and from the Nile to the Oxus and beyond, nowhere else had such an experiment in popular sovereignty even been imagined, let alone attempted.

The Riddah Wars—632–634 C.E.

Abu Bakr's was a short but highly successful reign—only two and a half years. His principal achievement as Caliph was his military campaigns against the "false prophets" and those tribes who had ceased paying the zakat, or tithe tax, because, in true tribal fashion, they considered Muhammad's death to have annulled their oath of allegiance. Recognizing that the defection of these tribes would greatly weaken the political stability of the Ummah and economically devastate the small Muslim régime in Medina, Abu Bakr sent his armies to deal ruthlessly with the rebels. The Riddah Wars, as these campaigns came to be known, sent a powerful message to the Arab tribes that their pledge had been made not to any mortal Shaykh but to the immortal community of God, making the pledge's retraction both an act of treason against the Ummah and a sin against God.

The Riddah Wars represented Abu Bakr's conscious effort to maintain the unity of the Arabs under the eternal banner of Islam and the centralized authority of Medina, and thus to prevent Muhammad's community from dissolving back into the old tribal system. But these must not be mistaken for religious wars; the campaigns were intended to reinforce the purely political interests of Medina. Still, the Riddah Wars did have the regrettable consequence of permanently associating apostasy (denying one's faith) with treason (denying the central authority of the Caliph).

Like territorial expansion and religious proselytization, apostasy and treason were nearly identical terms in seventh-century Arabia. However, the relationship between the two has endured in Islam, so that even today, there are some Muslims who continue to make the unsubstantiated and un-Quranic assertion that the two sins—apostasy and treason—deserve the same punishment: death. It is this belief that has given the *Ulama* (scriptural scholars) in some Muslim countries the authority to impose capital punishment on apostates, by whom they mean anyone who disagrees with their particular interpretation of Islam.

Abu Bakr is remembered for one other decision that he made as Caliph. Claiming once to have heard Muhammad say, "We [the Prophets] do not have heirs. Whatever we leave is alms," the Caliph disinherited Ali and Fatima from Muhammad's property. Henceforth, the family of the Prophet was to be fed and clothed only through alms provided by the community. Given that there were no other witnesses to Muhammad's statement, this was a remarkable decision. But what makes the decision even more curious is that Abu Bakr generously provided for Muhammad's wives by giving them the Prophet's house as a bequest. He even gave his own daughter, Aisha, some of Muhammad's former property in Medina.

Abu Bakr's actions are often interpreted as an attempt to weaken the Banu Hashim and strip the family of Muhammad of their privileged status as Muhammad's kin. But it also seems likely that in both providing for Muhammad's wives and ensuring that their purity would remain inviolate, Abu Bakr was signaling to the community that it was Aisha and the rest of the Mothers of the Faithful who were truly the family of Muhammad.

Ali was stunned by Abu Bakr's decision, but he accepted his fate without argument. Fatima, on the other hand, was inconsolable. In the span of a few months, she had lost her father, her inheritance, and her livelihood. She never spoke to Abu Bakr again, and when she died a short time later, Ali quietly buried her at night without bothering to inform the Caliph.

Scholars have long argued that there must have been some other motivation behind Abu Bakr's decision to disinherit Ali and strip the family of Muhammad of power. Throughout his short Caliphate, Abu Bakr seemed to do everything in his power to prevent Ali from ever attaining a position of authority in the Ummah, mostly because of his conviction that prophethood and Caliphate—that is, religious and secular authority—should not rest in a single clan, lest the two become indistinguishable. But to say that there was no personal animosity between Abu Bakr and Ali would be a lie. Even while Muhammad was alive, there was a great deal of friction between the two men.

The schism between the two widened further when, without any consultation whatsoever, Abu Bakr decided to appoint Umar as his successor rather than call for another shura. The only plausible explanation for Abu Bakr's surprising decision was that he must have believed a shura would revive the debate over the rights of the family of the Prophet. Indeed, a shura might have led to the succession of Ali, who had, over the past two years, become increasingly popular. The support he already enjoyed from a number of influential clans and Companions could very well have led uncommitted clans to back his candidacy. Granted, the vested interests of the Quraysh aristocracy in maintaining the status quo would not have made Ali's selection certain. But had it come to a contest between the enormously popular Ali and the fiery, rigid, and, by all accounts, misogynistic Umar, the latter would not have been assured of victory. To avoid that outcome, Abu Bakr ignored both tribal tradition and Muslim precedent, and simply handpicked Umar, though, again, the new Caliph had to be approved by the consensus of the community.

Umar ibn al-Khattab Succeeds Abu Bakr—634 c.e.

As Caliph, Umar was exactly what Muhammad had always considered him to be: a brilliant and energetic leader. A warrior at heart, he maintained the Caliphate as a secular position but emphasized his role as war leader by adopting the additional title *Amir al-Mu' manin,* "the Commander of the Faithful." His superior skills in battle led to the defeat of the Byzantine army in southern Syria in 634 and the capture of Damascus a year later. With the help of the oppressed Syrian Jewish community, whom he had freed from Byzantine control, Umar then devastated the Iranian forces at Qadisiyyah on his way to subduing the great Sasanian Empire. Egypt and Libya fell easily to Umar's army, as did Jerusalem: the crowning achievement of his military campaigns.

Surprisingly, Umar proved to be a far better diplomat than anyone could have imagined. Recognizing the importance of appeasing the non-Arab converts, who even in his time were beginning to outnumber the Arabs, the Caliph treated his vanquished enemies as equal members of the Ummah and strove to eliminate all ethnic differences between Arab and non-Arab. The wealth that poured into Medina as a result of his military victories was distributed proportionately to everyone in the community, including the children. Umar went out of his way to curb the power of the former Quraysh aristocracy and strengthened his central authority by appointing governors, or *amirs,* to administer the Muslim provinces both near and far. At the same time, he gave his amirs strict instructions to respect the existing traditions and mores of the provinces, and not to attempt any radical changes in the way the local peoples had been previously governed. He reorganized the taxation system, bringing immense prosperity to the Ummah, and created a standing army of trained soldiers who were garrisoned away from the provinces so as not to disturb the local communities.

Umar even tried to heal the rift with Ali by reaching out to the Banu Hashim. Though he refused to return Ali's inheritance, he did hand over Muhammad's estates in Medina as an endowment to be administered by the family of Muhammad. He connected himself to the Banu Hashim by marrying Ali's daughter, and encouraged Ali's participation in his government by regularly consulting him on important matters. In fact, Umar rarely did anything without consulting a cadre of influential Companions that he kept around him at all times. This may have been because he recognized that his position as Caliph, though sanctioned by the Ummah, had not been achieved through traditional means. He was therefore keen to avoid seeming despotic in his judgments.

Despite his attempts to reach out to the Banu Hashim, however, Umar continued to uphold, as a matter of religious dogma, the contention that prophethood and the Caliphate should not reside in the same clan. Indeed, acknowledging the contention and accepting Muhammad's statement about having no heirs became for Umar part of the oath of allegiance. Like Abu Bakr, Umar was convinced that such power in the Banu Hashim would be detrimental to the Muslim community. Nevertheless, he could not ignore Ali's rising popularity.

Uthman ibn Affan Succeeds Umar—644 C.E.

Not wishing to make the same mistake as Abu Bakr and so further alienate the Banu Hashim, Umar refused to handpick a successor, choosing instead to gather a traditional shura. On his deathbed, Umar brought together the six leading candidates for the Caliphate, including, at last, Ali, and gave them three days to decide among themselves who would lead the community after his death. It was not long before only two men remained: Ali, the scion of the Banu Hashim, and a somewhat unremarkable seventy-year-old man named Uthman ibn Affan.

A wealthy member of the Umayyad clan—the clan of Muhammad's fiercest enemies, Abu Sufyan and Hind—Uthman was a Quraysh through and through. Although an early convert to Islam, he had never exhibited any leadership qualities; he was a merchant, not a warrior. Muhammad had deeply loved Uthman but had never once entrusted him with leading a raid or an army on his behalf, something nearly every other man standing at the shura had done on more than one occasion. It was precisely his inexperience and lack of political ambition that made Uthman such an attractive choice. He was, more than anything else, the perfect alternative to Ali: a prudent, reliable old man who would not rock the boat.

In the end, Ali and Uthman were each asked two questions by Abd al-Rahman, who, despite being Uthman's brother-in-law, had been selected as Hakam between the two men. First, would each man rule according to the principles of the Quran and the example of Muhammad? Both replied that they would. The second question was unexpected. Would each man, if selected Caliph, strictly follow the precedents set by the two previous Caliphs, Abu Bakr and Umar?

Not only was this a totally unprecedented requirement for leading the community, it was obviously meant to weed out one candidate in particular. For while Uthman remarked that he would follow the example of his predecessors in all his decisions as Caliph, Ali gave the men in the room a hard stare and answered flatly, "No." He would follow only God and

85

his own judgment. Ali's answer sealed the verdict. Uthman became the third Caliph and, in 644 C.E., was promptly endorsed by the Ummah.

The Banu Hashim had fumed when Ali was skipped over in favor of Abu Bakr. But Abu Bakr was a highly respected Muslim with impeccable credentials. Then the Hashim had been furious with Abu Bakr for ignoring Ali and simply choosing Umar as his successor. But, again, Umar was a strong leader and, without the proper channels, there was little they could do but voice their opposition. However, when Uthman was chosen as Caliph over Ali, the Banu Hashim had simply had enough.

It was perfectly clear to many in the community that Uthman's Caliphate was a deliberate attempt to accommodate the old Quraysh aristocracy, who were eager to regain their previous status as the elites of Arab society. With Uthman's selection, the House of Umayya was once again in charge of the Hijaz, just as it had been before Muhammad conquered it in the name of Islam. The irony of pledging allegiance to the clan of Muhammad's former enemies was not lost on the family of Muhammad. To make matters worse, rather than trying to heal the ever-widening rift in the community, Uthman only exacerbated the situation through his unabashed nepotism and inept leadership.

First, Uthman replaced nearly all of the existing amirs throughout the Muslim lands with members of his immediate family, as though signaling to everyone the preeminence of his clan. Then, he dipped regularly into the public treasury to dole out huge sums of money to his relatives. Finally, and most dramatically, he broke with tradition by giving himself the hitherto unthinkable title *Khalifat Allah:* "Successor to

God," a title that Abu Bakr had explicitly rejected. To Uthman's many enemies, this decision was a sign of his self-aggrandizement. The Caliph, it seemed, was regarding himself not as the deputy of the Messenger but as the representative of God on earth.

Uthman's actions made him a fiercely hated figure. Not only did the Banu Hashim and the Ansar turn against the Caliph, so did some of the Umayya's rival clans—the Banu Zuhra, the Banu Makhzum, and the Abd Shams—together with some of the most influential Companions, including Aisha and even Abd al-Rahman, Uthman's brother-in-law and the man who, as arbiter in the shura, had been instrumental in giving him the Caliphate in the first place. By the end of his rule, Uthman had made so many reckless decisions that not even his most significant accomplishment—the collection and canonization of the Quran—could enable him to escape the ire of the Muslim community.

In Muhammad's lifetime, the Quran was never collected in a single volume; in fact, it was never collected at all. As each individual recitation poured out of the Prophet's mouth, it was diligently memorized by a new class of scholars, personally instructed by Muhammad, called the *Qurra,* or "Quran readers." Only the most important recitations—those dealing with legal issues—were ever written down, primarily on bits of bone, scraps of leather, and the ribs of palm leaves.

After the Prophet's death, the Qurra dispersed throughout the community as the authorized teachers of the Quran. But with the rapid growth of the Ummah and the passing of the first generation of Quran readers, certain deviations began to appear in the various recitations. These were mostly insignificant differences reflecting the local and cultural affinities of Muslim communities in Iraq, or Syria, or Basra; they were immaterial to the meaning and message of the Quran. Nevertheless, the Medinan establishment became increasingly alarmed by these discrepancies and so began plans to do what Muhammad had never bothered doing: to create a single, codified, uniform text of the Quran.

Some traditions claim that the Quran, in its present form, was collected by Abu Bakr during his Caliphate. Most scholars, however, agree that it was Uthman who, in his capacity as the Successor to God, authorized a single universally binding text of the Quran in about 650 C.E. But in doing so, Uthman once again managed to alienate important members of the community when he decided to round up the variant collections of the Quran, bring them to Medina, and set fire to them.

This decision infuriated the leading Muslims of Iraq, Syria, and Egypt, not because they felt their Qurans were somehow better or more complete than Uthman's—as mentioned, the variations were quite inconsequential—but because they felt that Uthman was overstepping the bounds of his secular authority as Caliph. Uthman's response to their grievances was to brand as unbelievers anyone who questioned the authority of the official collection.

Agitation against Uthman reached its peak in 655, with revolts breaking out throughout the Muslim lands against the Caliph's incompetent and often corrupt amirs. In Medina, Uthman was openly despised. Once, while leading the Friday prayers at the mosque, he was showered with stones hurled from the back of the congregation. A stone hit him in the forehead and he tumbled off the minbar, falling unconscious to the floor. Eventually, the situation became so dire that a number of prominent Companions from Mecca banded together to beg the Caliph to recall his corrupt governors, cease his nepotism, and repent before the entire community. However, members of his own clan, and especially his influential and power-hungry cousin, Marwan, pressured Uthman not to look weak by humbling himself.

Things came to a violent end for Uthman a year later, when a massive delegation from Egypt, Basra, and Kufa marched to Medina to present their grievances directly to the Caliph. While refusing to receive the delegation personally, Uthman sent Ali to ask them to return to their homes with the promise that their grievances would be addressed.

What happened next is unclear; the sources are muddled and contradictory. Somehow, on their way back home, the Egyptian delegation intercepted a messenger carrying an official letter that demanded the immediate punishment of the rebel leaders for their insubordination. The letter was signed with the seal of the Caliph. Enraged, the delegation reversed course and returned to Medina, where, with the aid of the Basran and Kufan rebels, they laid siege to Uthman's home, trapping the Caliph inside.

Most historians are convinced that Uthman did not write that letter: He may have been a poor political leader, but he was not suicidal. He must have known the rebel leaders would not have accepted their punishment without a fight.

The most likely culprit was probably Marwan, who many in Uthman's own circle believed had written the letter. It was Marwan who had advised Uthman to deal harshly with the rebels when they first arrived with their grievances. It was Marwan's influence that kept Uthman from repenting of his more detrimental actions, like heaping riches upon his family from the public treasury. In fact, when the Companions criticized Uthman for precisely this kind of behavior, Marwan, who benefited most richly from Uthman's nepotism, drew his sword and threatened to kill the most respected members of the Ummah in the presence of the Prophet's successor.

Regardless of who wrote the letter, the Egyptian, Basran, and Kufan rebels—and nearly everyone else in Medina—believed that Uthman, according to all customs, had failed in his leadership and must, as a result, voluntarily step down as Caliph. He had, in one sense, forfeited his oath of allegiance as Shaykh of the Ummah and had violated Abu Bakr's declaration that if the Caliph neglects the laws of God and the Prophet, he has no right to obedience.

Yet, even as nearly everyone had turned against him, Uthman still refused to give up power. As far as he understood, his position as Khalifat Allah had been bestowed upon him by God, not by man; only God could remove the mantle of leadership from him. However, as a pious Muslim, Uthman refused to attack the rebels who besieged him, hoping he could maintain control of the Caliphate without shedding Muslim blood. He therefore commanded his supporters not to fight but to go home and wait for order to be restored naturally. However, it was far too late for that.

The rebels, provoked by a scuffle outside Uthman's home, stormed into the Caliph's inner chamber, where they found him sitting on a cushion, reading from the Quran that he himself had collected and codified. Ignored by the Companions and virtually unchallenged by the guards, the rebels asked him one final time to abdicate. When Uthman refused, the rebels drew their swords and plunged them into Uthman's chest. The Caliph fell forward upon the open Quran, his blood soaking into its gold-leafed pages.

Ali ibn Abi Talib Succeeds Uthman—656 C.E.

The Caliph's murder at the hands of fellow Muslims threw the Ummah into pandemonium. With the rebels still in control of Medina, it was unclear what would happen next. There were more than a few Muslims in the Hijaz who would have leaped at the opportunity to succeed Uthman, including two of the most prominent Meccan Companions, Talha ibn Ubayd Allah and Zubayr ibn al-Awwam, both of whom had been singled out for their piety by Muhammad.

And, of course, there was Ali.

When he heard of Uthman's assassination, Ali was in the mosque praying. Sensing the chaos that would result, he quickly returned home to look after his family, and especially to find his son Hasan, who had stayed behind to try to protect Uthman. The following day, when a fragile peace had settled over the city, Ali returned to the mosque to find a substantial delegation of Muslims beseeching him to accept the oath of allegiance and become the next Caliph. For nearly a quarter of a century, Ali had been pursuing the Caliphate. But now that it was being handed to him, he refused to accept it.

Given the circumstances, Ali's reluctance was not surprising. If the demise of Uthman had proved anything, it was that some form of popular consent was still vital to maintaining the authority of the Caliphate. But with the rebels in control of Medina, Egypt and Iraq in revolt, Mecca calling for the Caliphate to be restored to the original vision of Abu Bakr and Umar, and the Banu Umayya demanding immediate retribution for Uthman's death, popular sanction would have been impossible to achieve.

There was still a very large and formidable contingent of Muslims whose unconditional support for Ali had not waned over the years. This faction consisted of members of the Ansar, the Banu Hashim, some prominent clans of the Quraysh, a few leading Companions, and several large bodies of non-Arab Muslims (especially in Basra and Kufa) who together were loosely labeled *Shi'atu Ali,* the "Party of Ali": the *Shi'ah.*

Despite this support, it was not until his political rivals in Mecca, including Talha and Zubayr, promised to pledge him their allegiance that Ali finally succumbed and accepted the mantle of leadership. Insisting that the oath of allegiance be given publicly in the mosque and in the presence of the entire Medinan community, Ali ibn Abi Talib, cousin and son-in-law to the Prophet, finally took his place at the head of the Ummah. Significantly, Ali refused the title of Caliph, which he believed had been permanently tainted by Uthman. Instead, he opted for Umar's epithet, Amir al-Mu'manin, "Commander of the Faithful."

With the backing of his party, Ali restored order to Medina by announcing a general amnesty to all who had, in one way or another, played a role in Uthman's death. This was to be a time of forgiveness and reconciliation, not of retribution. The old tribal ways, Ali claimed, were over. He further appeased the rebellious territories by removing nearly all of Uthman's kin from their posts as amirs and filling the vacancies with qualified local leaders. Yet Ali's actions, especially his amnesty of the rebels, not only enraged the Umayya, they paved the way for Aisha to rally support in Mecca against the new

Caliph by pinning him with the responsibility for Uthman's murder.

Aisha did not really believe Ali was responsible for Uthman's death; even if she had, it is unlikely she would have cared. Aisha loathed Uthman and played a significant role in the rebellion against him. In fact, her brother, Muhammad, was instrumental in the Caliph's assassination. But having learned from her father, Abu Bakr, never to entrust the ahl al-bayt with the Caliphate, lest the distinction between religious and political authority in the Ummah become confused, Aisha saw Uthman's murder as a means to replace Ali with someone she considered more suitable for the position, most likely her close allies Talha or Zubayr. It was with the help of these two men that she organized a massive contingent of Meccans and, riding atop a camel, personally led them into battle against Ali's forces in Medina.

The Battle of the Camel, as it came to be known, was Islam's first experience of civil war, or *fitnah*. In some ways, this conflict was the inevitable result, not just of the continuing antagonism between the factions of Ali and Aisha, but of a steadily evolving debate within the community over the role of the Caliph and the nature of the Ummah. Too often, this debate has been portrayed as strictly polarized between those who considered the Caliphate to be a purely secular position and those who believed it should encompass both the temporal and religious authority of the Prophet. But this simple dichotomy masks the diversity of religio-political views that existed in seventh- and eighth-century Arabia about the nature and function of the Caliphate.

The astonishingly rapid expansion of Islam into what had to this point been considered the impregnable domains of the

Byzantine and Sasanian empires was, for most Muslims, proof of God's divine favor. At the same time, the encounter with foreign peoples and governments was forcing these Muslims to reexamine the ideals that governed the political structure of the community. And while everyone agreed that the Ummah could remain united only under the authority of a single leader, there was still no consensus as to who that leader should be and almost no agreement as to how that leader should lead.

On the one hand, there were Muslims like Aisha and her faction who, while recognizing the importance of building a community dedicated to the commandments of God, were nonetheless committed to maintaining the secular character of the Caliphate. This faction was referred to as the *Shi'atu Uthman,* "the Party of Uthman," though one should remember that Aisha in no way considered herself as advancing the cause of Uthman, whom she considered to have blighted the Caliphate established by her father and his protégé, Umar.

On the other hand, there was the Banu Umayya, who, in light of Uthman's lengthy reign as Caliph, had fallen under the impression that the Caliphate was now the hereditary property of their clan. It was for this reason that, upon Uthman's death, his closest kin, Mu'awiyah, the amir of Damascus and the scion of Umayya, decided to disregard the events taking place in Medina and instead begin plans to take over the Caliphate himself. In some ways, the *Shi'atu Mu'awiyah,* as this faction was called, represented the traditional ideal of tribal leadership, though Mu'awiyah himself seemed to be trying to steer the Ummah in the direction of the great empires of the Byzantines and Sasanians. No one was yet calling for the establishment of a Muslim kingdom, but it was becoming increasingly clear that the Ummah was now too large and too wealthy to maintain its unity according to the "neo-tribal" system established by Muhammad in Medina.

At the opposite end of the spectrum were the Shi'atu Ali, who were committed to preserving Muhammad's original vision of the Ummah, no matter the social or political consequences. Although it is true that some factions within this group thought the Caliphate should incorporate Muhammad's religious authority, it would be a mistake to consider this view the established *Shi'ite* position it would eventually become. At this point, there were no significant religious differences between the Shi'ah and the rest of the Muslim community, later called the *Sunni,* or "orthodox." The Party of Ali was nothing more than a political faction that maintained the right of the family of Muhammad to rule the community in Muhammad's stead.

However, there was a small faction within the Shi'ah who held the more extreme view that the Ummah was a divinely founded institution that could be run only by the most pious person in the community, irrespective of his tribe, lineage, or ancestry. Eventually called the Kharijites, this was the faction that justified Uthman's murder on the grounds that he had broken the commands of God and rejected the example of the Prophet, making him no longer worthy of the Caliphate. Because the Kharijites stressed the need for a religious authority as Caliph, they are often credited with being the first Muslim theocrats. But this was a tiny, fractious group whose radically theocratic position was rejected by nearly every other faction vying for control of the Muslim community.

What makes the Kharijites so important to Islamic history,

however, is that they represent the first self-conscious attempts at defining a distinctive Muslim identity. This was a group obsessed with establishing who could and could not be considered a Muslim. According to the Kharijites, anyone who disobeyed any of the Quranic prescriptions, or violated the example of the Prophet Muhammad in any way, was to be considered a *kafir*, or "unbeliever," and immediately expelled from the Ummah.

Small as this group may have been, they made a lasting contribution to Muslim thought by arguing that salvation comes solely through membership in the Ummah, which they considered to be the charismatic and divine community of God. They divided all Muslims into two camps: the "People of Heaven," as the Kharijites referred to themselves, and the "People of Hell," by whom they meant everyone else. In this respect, the Kharijites can be considered the first Muslim extremists, and although the group itself lasted only a couple of centuries, its austere doctrines were adopted by succeeding generations of extremists to give religious sanction to their political rebellions against both Muslim and non-Muslim governments.

Finally, it is important to recognize that, regardless of their views on the nature and function of the Caliphate, no Muslim in seventh-century Arabia would have recognized the distinction our modern societies make between the secular and the religious. The primary philosophical difference between the Shi'atu Uthman and the Kharijites, for instance, was not whether but to what extent religion should play a role in the governing of the state. Thus, while the Shi'atu Ali, the Shi'atu Uthman, the Shi'atu Mu'awiyah, and the Kharijites were above all else political factions, all four of these groups were also described in more religiously oriented terms by the use of the word *din,* or "religion."

It is difficult to discern where Ali fit into this debate over the nature and function of the Caliphate because, as will shortly become apparent, he never had a chance to fully embrace the position. It seems clear from the decisions he made upon succeeding Uthman that Ali agreed with the Kharijite position that the Ummah was a divinely inspired community that could no longer abide either by the imperial ideals of the Shi'atu Mu'awiyah or by the neo-tribal precedents of Abu Bakr and Umar as envisioned by the Shi'atu Uthman. Whether Ali thought the Caliphate should fully encompass Muhammad's religious authority is another matter.

Ali was certainly no Kharijite. But he felt deeply his connection to the Prophet, whom he had known his entire life. The two men grew up together as brothers in the same household, and Ali rarely left Muhammad's side either as a child or as an adult. So it would have been understandable if Ali believed his relationship with Muhammad gave him both the religious and political qualities necessary to lead God's divine community on the path marked out by the Prophet. But this does not mean Ali considered himself to be divinely appointed to continue Muhammad's prophetic function, as his followers would eventually claim, nor does it mean he believed that the Caliphate should necessarily be a religious position.

Considering the cunning political maneuvering taking place around Ali, his attempts to reshape the Caliphate into a position of religious piety, if not religious authority, seem doomed from the start. Nevertheless, Ali was committed to uniting the Ummah under the banner of the family of Muhammad and in accordance with Muhammad's egalitarian principles. Therefore, after his forces quickly overwhelmed Aisha's army at the Battle of the Camel—during which Talha and Zubayr were killed and Aisha seriously wounded by an arrow—rather than punish the rebels as Abu Bakr had done after the Riddah Wars, Ali rebuked, then pardoned Aisha and her entourage, allowing them to return to Mecca unmolested.

The Battle of Siffin—657 C.E.

With Mecca and Medina finally subdued, Ali transferred his Caliphate to Kufa in order to turn his attention to Mu'awiyah, who, as the son of Abu Sufyan and the cousin of Uthman, had appealed to the old tribal sentiments of his Qurayshi kinsmen to raise an army against Ali in retribution for Uthman's murder. In 657 C.E., Ali and his Kufan army met Mu'awiyah and his Syrian army at a place called Siffin. After a long and bloody battle, Ali's forces were on the verge of victory when, sensing defeat, Mu'awiyah ordered his army to raise copies of the Quran on their spears: a message signaling his desire to surrender for arbitration.

Most of Ali's army, and especially the Kharijite faction who had, to this point, remained loyal to him, pleaded with Ali to ignore the gesture and continue the battle until the rebels had been punished for their insubordination. But, though Ali sensed treachery on Mu'awiyah's part, he refused to ignore God's command that "if [the enemy] desists, then you must also cease hostilities" (2:193). Ordering his army to lay down their weapons, Ali accepted Mu'awiyah's surrender and called for a Hakam to settle the dispute between them.

This was a fatal decision. The arbitration that followed the Battle of Siffin declared Uthman's murder to have been unjust and worthy of retribution: a decision that, at least on the surface, seemed to justify Mu'awiyah's rebellion. However, far more ominous was the fact that the Kharijites considered Ali's decision to submit to arbitration rather than mete out God's justice upon the rebels to be a grave sin worthy of expulsion from the holy community. Crying "No judgment but God's," the Kharijites angrily abandoned Ali on the battlefield before the arbitration had even begun.

Ali barely had time to absorb the impact of the arbitration. After Siffin, he was reluctantly forced to send his army to deal with the Kharijites who had seceded from his party. No sooner had he subdued the Kharijites than he had to turn his attention back toward Mu'awiyah, who, during the lengthy arbitration process, had managed to reassemble his forces, capture Egypt, and, in 660 C.E., proclaim himself Caliph in Jerusalem. With his armies scattered and his supporters divided along ideological lines, Ali mustered what forces he had left and, the following year, prepared a final campaign against Mu'awiyah and the Syrian rebels.

Ali Is Murdered—661 C.E.

The morning before the campaign against Mu'awiyah was to begin, Ali entered the mosque in Kufa to pray. There he was met by Abd al-Rahman ibn 'Amr ibn Muljam, a Kharijite, who pushed his way through the crowded mosque, shouting, "Judgment belongs to God, Ali, not to you."

Drawing a poisoned sword, Ibn Muljam struck Ali on the head. It was a superficial wound, but the poison did its work.

Two days later, Ali died, and with him the dream of the Banu Hashim to unite the holy community of God under the single banner of the Prophet's family.

In a sermon delivered a few years before his assassination, Ali had remarked that "a virtuous man is recognized by the good that is said about him and the praises which God has destined him to receive from others." These were prescient words, for Ali may have died, but he was not forgotten. For millions of Shi'ah throughout the world, Ali remains the model of Muslim piety: the light that illuminates the straight path to God. He is, in the words of Ali Shariati, "the best in speech . . . the best in worship . . . the best in faith."

It is this heroic vision of Ali that has been firmly planted in the hearts of those who refer to the person they believe to have been the sole successor to Muhammad, not as the fourth Caliph but as something else, something more. Ali, the Shi'ah claim, was the first *Imam*: the "Proof of God on Earth."

The Caliphate After the Rightly Guided Ones

After Ali's death, Mu'awiyah was able to seize absolute control of all the Muslim lands. Moving the capital from Kufa to Damascus, Mu'awiyah inaugurated the Umayyad Dynasty, completing the transformation of the Caliph into a king, and the Ummah into an empire.

Mu'awiyah's Arab dynasty lasted a very short time, from 661 to 750 c.e. Ultimately, it was supplanted by the Abassid Dynasty, which was carried to power with the help of the non-Arab (mostly Persian) converts who so greatly outnumbered the Arab elites. The Abassids claimed descent from Muhammad's uncle al-Abass and rallied support from the Shi'ite

100

factions by moving their capital to Baghdad and massacring all the Umayya they could find. But the Shi'ah ultimately rejected Abassid claims of legitimacy and, as a result, were ruthlessly persecuted by the new Caliphs.

While continuing to rule as secular kings, the Abassid Caliphs embroiled themselves far more deeply in religious matters than had their Umayyad predecessors. The seventh Abassid Caliph, al-Ma'mun (d. 833), even attempted to impose a measure of imperial orthodoxy upon the Muslims under his rule by launching a short-lived, and ultimately unsuccessful, religious inquisition against those Ulama who disagreed with his theological beliefs.

Although their dynasty lasted well into the eleventh century, the later Abassid Caliphs were nothing more than figureheads who wielded no direct authority over the Muslim lands. Even Baghdad, their capital, was under the control of a Shi'ite conglomerate of aristocratic Iranian families called the *Buyids,* who from 932 to 1062 C.E. ran all affairs of state while still allowing the Abassid Caliph to remain on his powerless throne. Meanwhile, in Cairo, the Fatimids (909–1171)— Shi'ites who claimed descent from Ali's wife and Muhammad's daughter, Fatima—established themselves as Baghdad's rivals, maintaining political control over everything from Tunisia to Palestine. And in Spain, a lone descendant of the Umayya, Abd al-Rahman, who had managed to escape from the massacre that took place in Syria, founded his own dynasty that not only lasted well into the fifteenth century but became the paradigm of Muslim-Jewish-Christian relations.

The Persian Buyid chiefs were eventually replaced by the ethnic Turks who founded both the Ghaznavid Dynasty (977–1186), which claimed suzerainty over northeastern Iran,

Afghanistan, and northern India, and the Saljuq Dynasty (1038–1194), which ruled most of the lands east of that. It was the Turks who, infiltrating the various sultanates as hired militia, finally managed to reunite most of the Muslim lands under the single Caliphate of the Ottomans: the Sunni dynasty that ruled from their capital in Istanbul from 1453 until 1924, when they were displaced by the victors of World War I.

After the Caliphate

There is no longer any such thing as a Caliph. With the rise of the modern nation-state in the Middle East, Muslims have been struggling to reconcile their dual identities as both citizens of independent sovereign entities and members of a unified worldwide community.

Some have argued, a few of them violently, that the Caliphate should be restored as the emblem of Muslim unity. These Muslims believe that the ideals of Islam and nationalism are "diametrically opposed to each other," to quote Mawlana Mawdudi, founder of the Pakistani sociopolitical movement *Jama'at-i Islami* (the Islamic Association). Consequently, Mawdudi and many others feel that the only legitimate Islamic state would be a world-state "in which the chains of racial and national prejudices would be dismantled."

The twentieth century has witnessed a transformation of the historic contest over the function of the Caliph and the nature of the Ummah into a debate over the proper way to combine the religious and social principles of Islam—as defined by Muhammad and developed by the Rightly Guided

Ones—with modern ideals of constitutionalism and democratic rights. And yet, this contemporary debate remains deeply rooted in the same questions of religious and political authority with which the Ummah grappled during the first few centuries of Islam.

Thus, in 1934, the modernist reformer Ali Abd ar-Raziq (1888–1966) argued for the separation of religion and state in Egypt by drawing a clear distinction between the authority of the Prophet, which he believed was solely limited to his religious function as Messenger of God, and the purely secular function of the Caliphate, which was nothing more than a civil institution that all Muslims felt free to question, oppose, and even rise up against. Ar-Raziq claimed that the universality of Islam could be based only on its religious and moral principles, which have nothing to do with the political order of individual states.

Some years later, the Egyptian academic and activist Sayyid Qutb (1906–1966) countered ar-Raziq's argument by claiming that Muhammad's position in Medina encompassed both religious and political authority, making Islam a unity whose "theological beliefs [cannot be] divorced in nature or in objective from secular life." Therefore, the only legitimate Islamic state is that which addresses both the material and the moral needs of its citizens.

In the 1970s, the Ayatollah Ruhollah Khomeini applied a distinctly Shi'ite interpretation of Qutb's argument to assume control over a social revolution that was already under way against Iran's despotic American-backed monarchy. Appealing both to the historic sentiments of the country's Shi'ite majority and to the democratic aspirations of its disaffected masses, Khomeini argued that only a supreme religious authority could manage the "social and political affairs of the people in the same way as the Prophet [had done]."

All of these political leaders were, in one way or another, trying to restore some sense of unity to what has become a deeply fractured worldwide community of Muslims. Yet without either a centralized political authority (like a Caliph) or a centralized religious authority (like a Pope) to provide a single voice to unite the worldwide Muslim community, Islam has fractured into dozens of competing sects and schisms, with each group claiming the right to interpret the meaning and message of Islam for everyone else. The result has been a shouting match of sorts. And, as in any shouting match, it is often those who shout the loudest—the extremists, the fanatics, the violent, and the revolutionary—that ever get heard. That has certainly been the case these last few years, which have witnessed the rise of violent extremist groups like al-Qaeda who believe that their rigid and puritanical form of Islam is the only correct form of Islam, and that all other Muslims are unbelievers who must be converted to their beliefs or be destroyed.

But while the tragic events of September 11, 2001, have given rise to anti-Muslim sentiments across the world, they have also initiated a vibrant and much-needed discourse among Muslims themselves about how to reconcile their beliefs and practices with the realities of the modern world. In fact, what has occurred since that fateful day amounts to nothing short of another Muslim civil war—a *fitnah*—which, like the contest to define Islam after the Prophet's death, is tearing the Muslim community into opposing factions.

As long as there is such a thing as *religion*, there will always be men and women whose radical reinterpretations of their faith will be fueled by their extreme social and political agendas, just as there will always be those who will fight for peace, tolerance, and reason. But to take part in the debate over the future of Islam, especially when it comes to such tricky issues as the notion of jihad, the relationship between Muslims, Jews, and Christians, and the role of women in Islam, we need a better, more complete understanding of how the Prophet himself understood and responded to these issues.

6

The Meaning of Jihad: Definition and Origin

Islam has so often been portrayed, even by contemporary scholars, as "a military religion, [with] fanatical warriors, engaged in spreading their faith and their law by armed might," to quote historian Bernard Lewis, that the image of the Muslim horde charging wildly into battle like a swarm of locusts has become one of the most enduring stereotypes in the Western world. "Islam was never really a religion of salvation," wrote the eminent sociologist Max Weber. "Islam is a warrior religion." It is a religion that Samuel Huntington portrayed as steeped "in bloody borders."

This deep-rooted stereotype of Islam as a warrior religion has its origins in the papal propaganda of the Crusades, when Muslims were depicted as the soldiers of the Antichrist in blasphemous occupation of the Holy Lands (and, far more importantly, of the silk route to China). In the Middle Ages, while Muslim philosophers, scientists, and mathematicians were preserving the knowledge of the past and determining the scholarship of the future, a belligerent and deeply fractured Holy Roman Empire tried to distinguish itself from the Turks who were strangling it from all sides by labeling Islam "the religion of the sword," as though there were in that era a means of territorial expansion other than war. And as the European colonialists of the eighteenth and nineteenth centuries systematically plundered the natural resources of the Middle East and North Africa, inadvertently creating a rabid political and religious backlash that would produce what is now popularly called "Islamic fundamentalism," the image of the dreaded Muslim warrior, "clad in a long robe and brandishing his scimitar, ready to slaughter any infidel that might come his way," became a widely popular literary cliché. It still is.

Today, the traditional image of the Muslim horde has been more or less replaced by a new image: the Islamic terrorist, strapped with explosives, ready to be martyred for God, eager to take as many innocent people as possible with him. What has not changed, however, is the notion that Islam is a religion whose adherents have been embroiled in a perpetual state of holy war, or jihad, from the time of Muhammad to this very day.

Yet the doctrine of jihad, like so many doctrines in Islam, was not fully developed as an ideological expression until long after Muhammad's death, when Muslim conquerors began absorbing the cultures and practices of the Near East. Islam, it must be remembered, was born in an era of grand empires and global conquests, a time in which the Byzantines and Sasanians—both theocratic kingdoms—were locked in a permanent state of religious war for territorial expansion.

The Muslim armies that spread out of the Arabian Peninsula simply joined in the existing fracas; they neither created it nor defined it, though they quickly dominated it. Despite the common perception in the West, the Muslim conquerors did not force conversion upon the conquered peoples; indeed, they did not even encourage it. The fact is that the financial and social advantages of being an Arab Muslim in the eighth and ninth centuries were such that Islam quickly became an elite clique, which a non-Arab could join only through a complex process that involved becoming first the client of an Arab.

This was also an era in which religion and the state were one unified entity. No Jew, Christian, Zoroastrian, or Muslim of this time would have considered their religion to be rooted in the personal confessional experiences of individuals. Quite the contrary. Your religion was your ethnicity, your culture, and your social identity; it defined your politics, your economics, and your ethics. More than anything else, your religion was your *citizenship*. Thus, the Holy Roman Empire had its officially sanctioned and legally enforced version of Christianity, just as the Sasanian Empire had its officially sanctioned and legally enforced version of Zoroastrianism. In the Indian subcontinent, Vaisnava kingdoms (devotees of Vishnu and his incarnations) vied with Saiva kingdoms (devotees of Shiva) for territorial control, while in China, Buddhist rulers fought Taoist rulers for political ascendancy.

Throughout every one of these regions, but especially in the Near East, where religion explicitly sanctioned the state, territorial expansion was identical to religious proselytization. In other words, *every* religion was a "religion of the sword."

As the Muslim conquerors set about developing the meaning and function of war in Islam, they had at their disposal the highly developed and imperially sanctioned ideals of religious warfare as defined and practiced by the Sasanian and Byzantine empires. In fact, the term "holy war" originates not with Islam but with the Christian Crusaders who first used it to give theological legitimacy to what was in reality a battle for land and trade routes. "Holy war" was not a term used by Muslim conquerors, and it is in no way a proper definition of the word *jihad*. There are a host of words in Arabic that can be definitively translated as "war"; jihad is not one of them.

The word *jihad* literally means "a struggle," "a striving," or "a great effort." In its primary religious connotation (sometimes referred to as "the greater jihad"), it means the struggle of the soul to overcome the sinful obstacles that keep a person from God. This is why the word *jihad* is nearly always followed in the Quran by the phrase "in the way of God." However, because Islam considers this inward struggle for holiness and submission to be inseparable from the outward struggle for the welfare of humanity, jihad has more often been associated with its secondary connotation ("the lesser jihad"): that is, any exertion—military or otherwise—against oppression and tyranny. And while this definition of jihad has occasionally been manipulated by militants and extremists to give religious sanction to what are in actuality social and political agendas, that is not at all how Muhammad understood the term.

War, according to the Quran, is either just or unjust; it is never "holy." Consequently, jihad is best defined as a primitive "just-war theory": a theory born out of necessity and developed in the midst of a bloody and often chaotic war that erupted in 624 C.E. between Muhammad's small but growing community and the all-powerful, ever-present Quraysh.

It is true that some verses in the Quran instruct Muhammad

and his followers to "slay the polytheists wherever you confront them" (9:5); to "carry the struggle to the hypocrites who deny the faith" (9:73); and, especially, to "fight those who do not believe in God and the Last Day" (9:29). However, it must be understood that these verses were directed at the Quraysh and their clandestine partisans in Yathrib—*specifically* named in the Quran as "the polytheists" and "the hypocrites," respectively—with whom the Ummah was locked in a terrible war.

Nevertheless, these verses have long been used by Muslims and non-Muslims alike to suggest that Islam advocates fighting unbelievers until they convert. But this is not a view that either the Quran or Muhammad endorsed. This view was put forth during the height of the Crusades, and partly in response to them, by later generations of Islamic legal scholars who developed what is now referred to as "the classical doctrine of jihad": a doctrine that, among other things, partitioned the world into two spheres, the House of Islam (*dar al-Islam*) and the House of War (*dar al-Harb*), with the former in constant pursuit of the latter.

As the Crusades drew to a close and Rome's attention turned away from the Muslim menace and toward the Christian reform movements cropping up throughout Europe, the classical doctrine of jihad was vigorously challenged by a new generation of Muslim scholars. The most important of these scholars was Ibn Taymiyya (1263–1328), whose influence in shaping Muslim ideology is matched only by St. Augustine's influence in shaping Christianity. Ibn Taymiyya argued that the idea of killing nonbelievers who refused to convert to Islam—the foundation of the classical doctrine of jihad—not only defied the example of Muhammad but also violated one

110

of the most important principles in the Quran: that "there can be no compulsion in religion" (2:256). Indeed, on this point the Quran is adamant. "The truth is from your Lord," it says; "believe it if you like, or do not" (18:29). The Quran also asks rhetorically, "Can you compel people to believe against their will?" (10:100) Obviously not; the Quran therefore commands believers to say to those who do not believe, "To you your religion; to me mine" (109:6).

Ibn Taymiyya's rejection of the classical doctrine of jihad fueled the works of a number of Muslim political and religious thinkers in the eighteenth and nineteenth centuries. In India, Sayyid Ahmed Khan (1817–98) used Ibn Taymiyya's argument to claim that jihad could not be properly applied to the struggle for independence against British occupation because the British had not suppressed the religious freedom of India's Muslim community—a Quranic requirement for sanctioning jihad (as one can imagine, this was an unpopular argument in colonial India). Chiragh Ali (1844–95), a protégé of Ahmed Khan, and one of the first Muslim scholars to push Quranic scholarship toward rational contextualization, argued that the modern Muslim community could not take Muhammad's historical Ummah as a legitimate example of how and when to wage war, because that community developed in a time when the whole of the known world was in a state of permanent conflict. Early in the twentieth century, the Egyptian reformer Mahmud Shaltut (1897–1963) used Chiragh Ali's contextualization of the Quran to show that Islam outlaws not only wars that are not made in direct response to aggression, but also those that are not officially sanctioned by a qualified Muslim jurist, or *mujtahid*.

Over the last century, however, and especially after the

colonial experience gave birth to a new kind of Islamic radicalism in the Middle East, the classical doctrine of jihad has undergone a massive resurgence in the pulpits and classrooms of a few prominent Muslim intellectuals. In Iran, the Ayatollah Khomeini (1902–89) relied on a militant interpretation of jihad, first to energize the anti-imperialist revolution of 1979 and then to fuel his destructive eight-year war with Iraq. It was Khomeini's vision of jihad as a weapon of war that helped found the Islamic militant group Hizbullah, whose use of the tactic of suicide bombing launched an appalling new era of international terrorism.

In Saudi Arabia, Abdullah Yusuf Azzam (1941–89), professor of Islamic philosophy at King Abdulaziz University, used his influence among the country's disaffected youth to promote an uncompromisingly belligerent interpretation of jihad that, he argued, was incumbent on all Muslims. "Jihad and the rifle alone," Dr. Azzam proclaimed to his students. "No negotiations, no conferences, and no dialogues." Azzam's views laid the foundations for the Palestinian militant group Hamas, which has since adopted Hizbullah's tactics in their resistance against the Israeli occupation. His teachings had an exceptional impact on one student in particular: Osama bin Laden, who eventually put into practice his mentor's ideology by calling for a worldwide Muslim campaign of jihad against the West, leading to the deaths of thousands of innocent people.

Of course, these attacks are not defensive strikes against specific acts of aggression. They are not sanctioned by a qualified mujtahid. They make no differentiation between combatant and noncombatant. And they indiscriminately kill men, women, children, Muslim, and non-Muslim. In other words, they fall far short of the regulations imposed by Muhammad for a legitimate *jihadi* response, which is why, despite common perception in the West, they are so roundly condemned by the vast majority of the world's Muslims, including some of Islam's most militant and anti-American clerics, such as Shaykh Fadlallah, the spiritual leader of Lebanon's Hizbullah, and the radical Muslim televangelist Yusuf al-Qaradawi.

The fact is that nearly one out of five people in the world are Muslims. And while some of them may share bin Laden's grievances against the Western powers, very few share his interpretation of jihad. Indeed, despite the ways in which this doctrine has been manipulated to justify either personal prejudices or political ideologies, jihad is neither a universally recognized nor a unanimously defined concept in the Muslim world. It is true that the struggle against injustice and tyranny is incumbent on all Muslims. After all, if there were no one to stand up to despots and tyrants, then, as the Quran states, our "monasteries, churches, synagogues, and mosques—places where the name of God is honored—would all be razed to the ground" (22:40). But it is nevertheless solely as a *defensive* response to oppression and injustice, and only within the clearly outlined rules of ethical conduct in battle, that the Quranic vision of jihad is to be understood. For if, as political theorists claim, the determining factor of a "just war" is the establishment of specific regulations covering both *jus in bello* (justice *in* war) and *jus ad bellum* (justice *of* war), then there can be no better way to describe Muhammad's doctrine of jihad than as an ancient Arabian "just war" theory.

7

Muslim-Jewish Relations

Over the last few years, a number of books and articles have been published arguing that the current conflicts in the modern world between Muslims and Jews can be traced all the way back to the conflicts between Muhammad and the Jewish community in Arabia. This theory, which is sometimes presented as an incontestable doctrine in both Islamic and Judaic studies, is founded on the belief that Muhammad, who considered his message to be a continuation of the Judeo-Christian prophetic tradition, came to Medina fully expecting the Jews to confirm his identity as a prophet. Supposedly, to facilitate the Jews' acceptance of his prophetic identity, Muhammad connected his community to theirs by adopting a number of Jewish rituals and practices. Worried that the rejection by the Jews would somehow discredit his prophetic claims, Muhammad had no choice but to turn violently against them, separate his community from theirs, and, in the words of F. E. Peters, "refashion Islam as an alternative to Judaism."

There are two problems with this theory. First, it fails to appreciate Muhammad's own religious and political acumen. It is not as though the Prophet were an ignorant Bedouin worshipping the elements or bowing before slabs of stone. This was a man who, for nearly half a century, had lived in the religious capital of the Arabian Peninsula, where he was a sophisticated merchant with firm economic and cultural ties to both Jewish and Christian tribes. It would have been ridiculously naïve for Muhammad to assume that his prophetic mission would be as obvious to the Jews as it was to him. He would need only to have been familiar with the most rudimentary doctrine of Judaism to know that they would not have necessarily accepted his identity as one of their prophets. Certainly he was aware that the Jews did not recognize Jesus as a prophet; why would he have assumed they would recognize him as such?

The fact is that nothing Muhammad either said or did would necessarily have been objectionable to Medina's Jews. As Gordon Newby writes in *A History of the Jews of Arabia*, Islam and Judaism in seventh-century Arabia operated within "the same sphere of religious discourse," in that both shared the same religious characters, stories, and anecdotes, both discussed the same fundamental questions from similar perspectives, and both had nearly identical moral and ethical values. Where there was disagreement between the two faiths, Newby suggests it was "over interpretation of shared topics, not over two mutually exclusive views of the world." To quote S. D. Goiten, there was simply "nothing repugnant to the Jewish religion in Muhammad's preaching."

It would be simplistic to argue that no polemical conflict existed between Muhammad and the Jews of his time. But this conflict had far more to do with political alliances and economic ties than with a theological debate over scripture. This was a conflict fueled primarily by tribal partnerships and tax-free markets, not religious zeal. And while Muhammad's biographers like to present him as debating theology with belligerent groups of "rabbis" who show "hostility to the apostle in envy, hatred, and malice, because God had chosen His apostle from the Arabs," the similarities in both the tone and manner of these events and the stories of the quarrels Jesus had with the Pharisees points to their function as a literary device, not historical fact. Indeed, scholars have for centuries been aware of the intentional connection the early Muslims tried to draw between Jesus and Muhammad in an attempt to connect the mission and message of the two prophets.

Bear in mind, Muhammad's biographies were written at a time when the Jewish minority in the Muslim state was Islam's only remaining theological rival. It is not surprising, therefore, that Muslim historians and theologians would have buttressed their arguments against the rabbinical authorities of their time by planting their words in Muhammad's mouth. If Muhammad's biographies reveal anything at all, it is the anti-Jewish sentiments of the Prophet's biographers, not of the Prophet himself. To understand Muhammad's actual beliefs regarding the Jews and Christians of his time, one must look not to the words that chroniclers put into his mouth hundreds of years after his death, but rather to the words that God put into his mouth while he was alive.

The Quran, as a holy and revealed scripture, repeatedly reminds Muslims that what they are hearing is not a new message but the "confirmation of previous scriptures" (12:111). In fact, the Quran proposes the unprecedented notion that *all* revealed scriptures are derived from a single concealed book in heaven called the *Umm al-Kitab,* or "Mother of Books" (13:39). That means that as far as Muhammad understood, the Torah, the Gospels, and the Quran must be read as a single, cohesive narrative about humanity's relationship to God, in which the prophetic consciousness of one prophet is passed spiritually to the next: from Adam to Muhammad. For this reason, the Quran advises Muslims to say to the Jews and Christians: "We believe in God, and in that which has been revealed to us, which is that which was revealed to Abraham and Ismail and Jacob and the tribes [of Israel], as well as that which the Lord revealed to Moses and to Jesus and to all the other Prophets. We make no distinction between any of them; we submit ourselves to God" (3:84).

Muslims believe that the Quran is the final revelation in this sequence of scriptures, just as they believe Muhammad to be "the Seal of the Prophets." But the Quran never claims to annul the previous scriptures, only to complete them. And while the notion of one scripture giving authenticity to others is, to say the least, a remarkable event in the history of religions, the concept of the Umm al-Kitab may indicate an even more profound principle.

As the Quran suggests over and over again, and as the Constitution of Medina explicitly affirms, Muhammad may have understood the concept of the Umm al-Kitab to mean not only that the Jews, Christians, and Muslims shared a single divine scripture but also that they constituted a single divine Ummah. As far as Muhammad was concerned, the Jews and the Christians were "People of the Book" (*ahl al-Kitab*), spiritual cousins who, as opposed to the pagans and polytheists of Arabia, worshipped the same God, read the same scriptures, and shared the same moral values as his Muslim community.

Although each faith comprised its own distinct religious community (its own individual Ummah), together they formed one united Ummah, an extraordinary idea that Mohammed Bamyeh calls monotheistic pluralism. Thus, the Quran promises that "all those who believe—the Jews, the Sabians, the Christians—*anyone who believes in God and the Last Days, and who does good deeds, will have nothing to fear or regret*" (5:69; emphasis added).

It was this conviction of the existence of a unified, monotheistic Ummah that led Muhammad to connect his community to the Jews, not that he felt the need to emulate the Jewish clans, nor that he wanted to facilitate their acceptance of him as a prophet. Muhammad aligned his community with the Jews in Medina because he considered them, as well as the Christians, to be part of his Ummah. Consequently, when he came to Medina, he made Jerusalem—the site of the Temple (long since destroyed) and the direction in which the Diaspora Jews turned during worship—the direction of prayer, or *qiblah,* for all Muslims. He imposed a mandatory fast upon his community, which was to take place annually on the tenth day (*Ashura*) of the first month of the Jewish calendar, the day more commonly known as Yom Kippur. He purposely set the day of Muslim congregation at noon on Friday so that it would coincide with, but not disrupt, Jewish preparations for the Sabbath. He adopted many of the Jewish dietary laws and purity requirements, and encouraged his followers to marry Jews, as he himself did (5:5–7).

And while it is true that after a few years, Muhammad both changed the qiblah from Jerusalem to Mecca, and set the annual fast at Ramadan (the month in which the Quran was first revealed) instead of Yom Kippur, these decisions should not be interpreted as "a break with the Jews" but as the maturing of Islam into its own independent religion. Despite the changes, Muhammad continued to encourage his followers to fast on Yom Kippur, and he never ceased to venerate Jerusalem as a holy city; indeed, after Mecca and Medina, Jerusalem is the most sacred city in the whole of the Muslim world. Moreover, the Prophet maintained most of the dietary, purity, and marriage restrictions he had adopted from the Jews. And until the day he died, Muhammad continued to engage in peaceful discourse—not theological debate—with the Jewish communities of Arabia, just as the Quran had commanded him to do: "Do not argue with the People of the Book—apart from those individuals who act unjustly toward you—unless it is in a fair way" (29:46). Muhammad's example must have had a lasting effect on his early followers: As Nabia Abbott has shown, throughout the first two centuries of Islam, Muslims regularly read the Torah alongside the Quran.

Certainly, Muhammad understood that there were distinct theological differences between Islam and the other Peoples of the Book. But he saw these differences as part of the divine plan of God, who could have created a single Ummah if he had wanted to but instead preferred that "every Ummah have its own Messenger" (10:47). Thus, to the Jews, God sent the Torah, "which contains guidance and light"; to the Christians, God sent Jesus, who "confirms the Torah"; and finally, to the Arabs, God sent the Quran, which "confirms the earlier revelations." In this way, the ideological differences among the Peoples of the Book is explained by the Quran as indicating God's desire to give each people its own "law and path and way of life" (5:42–48).

That being said, there were some theological differences that Muhammad considered intolerably heretical innovations created by ignorance and error. Chief among these was the concept of the Trinity. "God is one," the Quran states definitively. "God is eternal. He has neither begotten anyone, nor is he begotten of anyone" (112:1–3).

Yet this verse, and the many others like it in the Quran, is in no way a condemnation of Christianity per se but of Imperial Byzantine (Trinitarian) Orthodoxy, which was neither the sole nor the dominant Christian position in the Hijaz. From the beginning of his ministry, Muhammad revered Jesus as the greatest of God's messengers. Much of the Gospel narrative is recounted in the Quran, though in a somewhat abridged version, including Jesus's virgin birth (3:47), his miracles (3:49), his identity as Messiah (3:45), and the expectation of his judgment over humanity at the end of time (4:159).

What the Quran does not accept, however, is the belief of Orthodox Trinitarians who argued that Jesus was *himself* God. These Christians Muhammad did not even consider to be Peoples of the Book: "It is the unbeliever who says, 'God is the third of three,'" the Quran declares. "There is only God the One!" (5:73). It was Muhammad's belief that Orthodox Christians had corrupted the original message of Jesus, who, the Quran contends, never claimed divinity and never asked to be worshipped (5:116–18) but rather commanded his disciples to "worship God, who is my Lord and your Lord" (5:72).

At the same time, Muhammad lashed out at those Jews in Arabia who had "forsaken the community of Abraham" (2:130) and "who were trusted with the laws of the Torah, but who fail to observe them" (62:5). Again, this was not a condemnation of Judaism. The respect and reverence that Muhammad had for the great Jewish patriarchs is evidenced by the fact that almost every biblical prophet is mentioned in the Quran. Rather, Muhammad was addressing those Jews in the Arabian Peninsula—and only in the Arabian Peninsula—who had in both belief and practice "breached their covenant with God" (5:13). And, if the Jewish clans in Medina were any indication, there were many of them.

Muhammad's complaints in the Quran were not directed against the religions of Judaism and Christianity, which he considered to be nearly identical to Islam: "We believe in what has been revealed to us, just as we believe in what has been revealed to you [Jews and Christians]," the Quran says. "Our God and your God are the same; and it is to Him we submit" (29:46). His complaint was against those Jews and Christians he had encountered in Arabia who, in his opinion, had forsaken their covenant with God and perverted the teachings of the Torah and Gospels. These were not believers but apostates with whom the Quran warns Muslims not to ally themselves: "O believers, do not make friends with those who mock you and make fun of your faith. . . . Instead say to them: 'O People of the Book, why do you dislike us? Is it because we believe in God and in what has been sent down to us [the Quran], and what was sent down before that [the

121

Torah and Gospels], while most of you are disobedient?'" (5:57–59)

The point is that when Muhammad reminded the Jews of Arabia of the "favors [God] bestowed on you, making you the most exalted nation in the world" (2:47), when he raged against the Christians for abandoning their faith and confounding the truth of their scriptures, when he complained that both groups "no longer follow the teachings of the Torah and the Gospel, and what has been revealed to them by their Lord" (5:66), he was merely following in the footsteps of the prophets who had come before him. He was, in other words, Isaiah calling his fellow Jews "a sinful nation, a people laden with iniquity, offspring of evildoers" (Isaiah 1:4); he was John the Baptist lashing out against "the brood of vipers" who assumed that their status as "sons of Abraham" would keep them safe from judgment (Luke 3:7–8); he was Jesus promising damnation for the hypocrites who "for the sake of tradition, have made void the word of God" (Matthew 15:6). After all, isn't this exactly the message a prophet is supposed to deliver?

Muhammad's example to his community explains why, for the most part, Jews thrived under Muslim rule, especially after Islam expanded into Byzantine lands, where Orthodox rulers routinely persecuted both Jews and non-Orthodox Christians for their religious beliefs, often forcing them to convert to Imperial Christianity under penalty of death. In contrast, Muslim law, which considers Jews and Christians "protected peoples" (*dhimmi*), neither required nor encouraged their conversion to Islam. Muslim persecution of the dhimmi was not only forbidden by Islamic law, it was in direct defiance of Muhammad's orders to his expanding armies never to trouble

Jews in their practice of Judaism, and always to preserve the Christian institutions they encountered.

In return for a special "protection tax" called *jizyah*, Muslim law allowed Jews and Christians both religious autonomy and the opportunity to share in the social and economic institutions of the Muslim world. Nowhere was this tolerance more evident than in medieval Spain—the supreme example of Muslim, Jewish, and Christian cooperation—where Jews were able to rise to the highest positions in society and government. One of the most powerful men in all of Muslim Spain was a Jew named Hasdai ibn Shaprut, who for many decades served as the trusted vizier to the Caliph Abd al-Rahman III. It is no wonder, then, that Jewish documents written during this period refer to Islam as "an act of God's mercy."

Of course, even in Muslim Spain, there were periods of intolerance and religious persecution. Moreover, Islamic law did prohibit Jews and Christians from openly proselytizing their faith in public places. But such prohibitions affected Christians more than they did Jews, who have been historically disinclined toward both proselytizing and public displays of their religious rituals. This may explain why Christianity gradually disappeared in most of the Islamic lands, while Jewish communities increased and prospered.

It is no coincidence that just as they reversed many of Muhammad's social reforms aimed at empowering women (see the next chapter), the Muslim scriptural and legal scholars of the following centuries rejected the notion that Jews and Christians were part of the Ummah, and instead designated both groups as unbelievers. These scholars reinterpreted the Revelation to declare that the Quran had superseded, rather than supplemented, the Torah and the Gospels, and called on Muslims to distinguish themselves from the People of the Book. This was largely an attempt to differentiate the nascent religion of Islam from other communities so it could establish its own religious independence.

Nevertheless, the actions of these scriptural scholars were in direct defiance of Muhammad's example and the teachings of the Quran. For even though Muhammad recognized the irreconcilable differences that existed among the Peoples of the Book, he never called for a partitioning of the faiths. It is a tragedy that after fourteen hundred years, this simple compromise has yet to overcome the sometimes petty yet often binding ideological differences between the three faiths of Abraham.

8

Women in Islam

Perhaps nowhere was Muhammad's struggle for economic re-
distribution and social egalitarianism more evident than in
the rights and privileges he bestowed upon the women in his
community. Beginning with the unbiblical conviction that
men and women were created together and simultaneously
from a single cell (4:1; 7:189), the Quran goes to great lengths
to emphasize the equality of the sexes in the eyes of God:

> God offers forgiveness and a great reward,
> For men who surrender to Him, and women who surrender
>   to Him,
> For men who believe, and women who believe,
> For men who obey, and women who obey,
> For men who speak truth, and women who speak truth,
> For men who persevere, and women who persevere,
> For men who are humble, and women who are humble,

For men who give alms, and women who give alms,
For men who fast, and women who fast,
For men who are modest, and women who are modest,
For men who remember God, and women who remember
    God. (33:35)

At the same time, the Quran acknowledges that men and women have distinct and separate roles in society; it would have been preposterous to claim otherwise in seventh-century Arabia. Thus, "men are to take care of women, because God has given them greater strength, and because men use their wealth to provide for them" (4:34).

With a few notable exceptions (like Khadija), women in pre-Islamic Arabia could neither own property nor inherit it from their husbands. A wife was herself considered property, and both she and her dowry would be inherited by the male heir of her deceased husband. If the male heir was uninterested in the widow, he could hand her over to his kin—a brother or a nephew—who could then marry her and take control of her dead husband's property. If she was too old to marry again, or if no one was interested in her, she and her dowry would revert to the clan. The same was true for all orphans who, like Muhammad when his parents died, were considered too young to inherit property from their fathers.

Muhammad, as noted in chapter four, completely upended this social order and gave Muslim women inheritance and divorce rights that their European and Christian counterparts would not enjoy for another thousand years. But perhaps the greatest change he made to the status of women was in curtailing the practice of polygamy.

In some ways, pre-Islamic Arabian custom was extraordinarily lax when it came to both marriage and divorce. In Bedouin societies, both men and women practiced polygamy and both had recourse to divorce: men simply by making a statement such as "I divorce you!" and women—who remained with their father's family during marriage—by turning their tent around so that its entrance would no longer be available to the husband when he came for a "visit." Because paternity was unimportant in Bedouin societies (lineage was passed primarily through the mother), it made no difference how many husbands a woman had or who fathered her children. However, in sedentary societies like Mecca, where the accumulation of wealth made inheritance and, therefore, paternity much more important, matrilineal society (that is, inherited or traced through the line of the mother) had gradually given way to a patrilineal one (that is, through the father). As a result of this trend toward patriliny, women in sedentary societies were gradually stripped of both their right to divorce and their access to polyandry, the practice of having more than one husband.

Although Muhammad's views on marriage seem far more influenced by Jewish tradition than by the traditions of pre-Islamic Arabia, he was still a product of Meccan society. So while he limited the rights of men to divorce their wives—forcing upon them a three-month reconciliation period before the statement of divorce could take effect—and while he provided women with the right to divorce their husbands if they feared "cruelty or ill-treatment" (4:128), he nonetheless consolidated the move toward a patrilineal society by putting a definitive end to all polyandrous unions. Never again could a Muslim woman have more than one husband. Whether a Muslim man may have more than one wife (polygyny), however, remains a contested issue to this day.

On the one hand, Muhammad clearly accepted polygyny (within limits) as necessary for the survival of the Ummah, especially after war with the Quraysh resulted in hundreds of widows and orphans who had to be provided for and protected by the community. "Marry those women who are lawful for you, up to two, three, or four," the Quran states, "but *only if you can treat them all equally*" (4:3; emphasis added).

On the other hand, the Quran makes it clear that monogamy is the preferred model of marriage when it asserts that "no matter how you try, *you will never be able to treat your wives equally*" (4:129; emphasis added). This seeming contradiction offers some insight into a dilemma that plagued the community during its early development. Essentially, while the individual believer was to strive for monogamy, the community that Muhammad was trying to build in Yathrib would have been doomed without polygyny.

For the vast majority of Muslims throughout the world, there is little doubt that the two verses cited above, when combined and considered in their historical context, should be interpreted as rejecting polygamy in all its forms. And yet, there are still those Muslims, especially in tribal societies like Saudi Arabia and Afghanistan, who continue to use the Quran and the example set by Muhammad to justify their polygamous marriages.

Unfortunately, not long after Muhammad's death, many of the radical advances in women's rights that he had spent his life and ministry advocating were systematically undermined by his own followers. The reversal in the role of women

Panera Bread
Cafe 1539
Chicago, IL 60602
Phone: 312-332-6895

Accuracy Matters.
Your order should be correct every time.
If it's not, we'll fix it right away, and
give you a free treat for your trouble.
Just let any associate know.

4/3/2016	1:57:17 PM

Check Number: 636462   Cashier: Brashay
1 Bwl Creamy Tomato Soup   5.29
          1 French Baguette
                SubTotal   5.29
                Tax   0.61
                Total   5.90
                Master Card   5.90
                Acct:XXXXXXXX2951
                AuthCode:91801P
                Trans#:8596
Log in at PaneraBread.com.
You are 2 visits away from your next reward

MyPanera Member: xxxxxxxxxxxx02005
MyPanera Offers Earned:
Visits to Next Reward: 2

www.panerabread.com

HERE POS
Your Order Number is: 662
Customer / Pager: Steven 54

Customer Copy

had partly to do with the circumstances faced by the Muslim community in the tumultuous years following Muhammad's death. This was an era in which the Ummah was growing and expanding in wealth and power at an astounding rate. A mere fifty years after the Prophet's passing, the tiny community that Muhammad had founded in Yathrib burst out of the Arabian Peninsula and swallowed whole the massive Sasanian Empire of Iran. Fifty years after that, it had secured most of northwest India, absorbed all of North Africa, and reduced the Christian Byzantine Empire to little more than a deteriorating regional power. Fifty years after that, Islam had pushed its way deep into Europe through Spain and southern France.

As Muhammad's small community of Arab followers swelled into the largest empire in the world, it faced a growing number of legal and religious challenges that were not explicitly dealt with in the Quran. While Muhammad was still in their midst, these questions could simply be brought to him. But without the Prophet, it became progressively more difficult to ascertain God's will on issues that far exceeded the knowledge and experiences of a group of Hijazi tribesmen.

At first, the Ummah naturally turned to the early Companions for guidance and leadership. As the first generation of Muslims—the people who had walked and talked with the Prophet—the Companions had the authority to make legal and spiritual decisions by virtue of their direct knowledge of Muhammad's life and teachings. They were the living repositories of the *hadith:* oral anecdotes recalling the words and deeds of Muhammad.

The hadith, insofar as they addressed issues not dealt with in the Quran, would become an indispensable tool in the formation of Islamic law. However, in their earliest stages, the hadith were muddled and totally unregulated, making their authentication almost impossible. Worse, as the first generation of Companions passed on, the community had to rely increasingly on the reports that the second generation of Muslims (known as the *Tabiun*) had received from the first; when the second generation died, the community was yet another step removed from the actual words and deeds of the Prophet.

Thus, with each successive generation, the "chain of transmission," or *isnad*, that was supposed to authenticate the hadith grew longer and more convoluted, so that in less than two centuries after Muhammad's death, there were already some seven hundred thousand hadith being circulated throughout the Muslim lands, the great majority of which were unquestionably fabricated by individuals who sought to legitimize their own particular beliefs and practices by connecting them with the Prophet. After a few generations, almost anything could be given the status of hadith if one simply claimed to trace its transmission back to Muhammad. In fact, the Hungarian scholar Ignaz Goldziher has documented numerous hadith the transmitters of which claimed were derived from Muhammad but which were in reality verses from the Torah and Gospels, bits of rabbinic sayings, ancient Persian maxims, passages of Greek philosophy, Indian proverbs, and even an almost word-for-word reproduction of the Lord's Prayer. By the ninth century, when Islamic law was being fashioned, there were so many false hadith circulating through the community that Muslim legal scholars somewhat whimsically classified them into two categories: lies told for material gain and lies told for ideological advantage.

In the ninth and tenth centuries, a concerted effort was made to sift through the massive accumulation of hadith to separate the reliable from the rest. Yet for hundreds of years, anyone who had the power and wealth necessary to influence public opinion on a particular issue—and who wanted to justify his own ideas about, say, the role of women in society—had only to refer to a hadith that he had heard from someone, who had heard it from someone else, who had heard it from a Companion, who had heard it from the Prophet.

It would be no exaggeration, therefore, to say that quite soon after Muhammad's death, those men who took upon themselves the task of interpreting God's will in the Quran and Muhammad's will in the hadith—men who were, coincidentally, among the most powerful and wealthy members of the Ummah—were not nearly as concerned with the accuracy of their reports or the objectivity of their exegesis as they were with regaining the financial and social dominance that the Prophet's reforms had taken from them. As the Islamic scholar Fatima Mernissi notes, one must always remember that behind every hadith lies the entrenched power struggles and conflicting interests that one would expect in a society "in which social mobility [and] geographical expansion [were] the order of the day."

Thus, when the Quran warned believers not to "pass on your wealth and property to the feeble-minded (*sufaha*)," the early Quranic commentators—all of them male—declared, despite the Quran's warnings on the subject, that "the *sufaha* are women and children . . . and *both of them must be excluded from inheritance*" (emphasis added).

When a wealthy and notable merchant from Basra named Abu Bakra (not to be confused with Abu Bakr) claimed, twenty-five years after Muhammad's death, that he once heard the Prophet say, "Those who entrust their affairs to a woman

131

will never know prosperity," his authority as a Companion was unquestioned.

When Abu Said al-Khudri swore he had heard the Prophet tell a group of women, "I have not seen anyone more deficient in intelligence and religion than you," his memory was unchallenged, despite the fact that Muhammad's biographers present him as repeatedly asking for and following the advice of his wives, even in military matters.

And finally, when the celebrated Quranic commentator Fakhr ad-Din ar-Razi (1149–1209) interpreted the verse "[God] created spouses for you of your own kind so that you may have peace of mind through them" (30:21) as "proof that women were created like animals and plants and other useful things [and not for] worship and carrying the Divine commands . . . because the woman is weak, silly, and in one sense like a child," his commentary became (and still is) one of the most widely respected in the Muslim world.

This last point bears repeating. The fact is that for fourteen centuries, the science of Quranic commentary has been the exclusive domain of Muslim men. And because each one of these exegetes inevitably brings to the Quran his own ideology and his own preconceived notions, it should not be surprising to learn that certain verses have most often been read in their most misogynistic interpretation. Consider, for example, how the following verse (4:34) regarding the obligations of men toward women has been rendered into English by two different but widely read contemporary translators of the Quran. The first is from the Princeton edition, translated by Ahmed Ali; the second is from Majid Fakhry's translation, published by New York University:

Men are the support of women [*qawwamuna 'ala an-nisa*] as God gives some more means than others, and because they spend of their wealth (to provide for them). . . . As for women you feel are averse, talk to them suasively; then leave them alone in bed (without molesting them) and go to bed with them (when they are willing).

Men are in charge of women, because Allah has made some of them excel the others, and because they spend some of their wealth. . . . And for those [women] that you fear might rebel, admonish them and abandon them in their beds and beat them [*adribuhunna*].

Because of the variability of the Arabic language, both of these translations are grammatically, syntactically, and definitionally correct. The phrase *qawwamuna 'ala an-nisa* can be understood as "watch over," "protect," "support," "attend to," "look after," or "be in charge of" women. The final word in the verse, *adribuhunna,* which Fakhry has rendered as "beat them," can equally mean "turn away from them," "go along with them," and, remarkably, even "have consensual intercourse with them." Which definition one chooses to accept and follow depends on what one is trying to extract from the text: if one views the Quran as empowering women, then Ali's; if one looks to the Quran to justify violence against women, then Fakhry's.

Throughout Islamic history, there have been a number of women who have struggled to maintain their authority as both preservers of the hadith and interpreters of the Quran. Karima bint Ahmad (d. 1069) and Fatima bint Ali (d. 1087), for example, are regarded as two of the most important transmitters of the Prophet's traditions, while Zaynab bint al-Sha'ri (d. 1220) and Daqiqa bint Murshid (d. 1345), both textual scholars, occupied an eminent place in early Islamic scholarship. And it is hard to ignore the fact that nearly one-sixth of all "reliable" hadith can be traced back to Muhammad's wife Aisha.

However, these women, celebrated as they are, were no match for the indisputable authority of early Companions like Umar, the young, brash member of the Quraysh elite whose conversion to Islam had always been a particular source of pride to Muhammad. The Prophet had always admired Umar, not just for his physical prowess as a warrior but for his impeccable moral virtue and the zeal with which he approached his devotion to God. In many ways, Umar was a simple, dignified, and devout man. But he also had a fiery temper and was prone to anger and violence, especially toward women. So infamous was he for his misogynistic attitude that when he asked for the hand of Aisha's sister, he was flatly rebuffed because of his rough behavior toward women.

Umar's misogynist tendencies were apparent from the moment he ascended to the leadership of the Muslim community. He tried (unsuccessfully) to confine women to their homes and wanted to prevent them from attending worship at the mosque. He instituted segregated prayers and, in direct violation of the Prophet's example, forced women to be taught by male religious leaders. Incredibly, he forbade Muhammad's widows to perform the pilgrimage rites and instituted a series of severe penal ordinances aimed primarily at women. Chief among these was the stoning to death of adulterers, a punishment that has absolutely no foundation whatsoever in the Quran but which Umar justified by claiming it had originally been part of the Revelation and had somehow been left out of the authorized text. Of course, Umar never explained how it was possible for a verse such as this "accidentally" to have been left out of the Divine Revelation of God, but then again, he didn't have to. It was enough that he spoke with the authority of the Prophet.

There is no question that the Quran, like all holy scriptures, was deeply affected by the cultural norms of the society in which it was revealed—a society that, as we have seen, did not consider women to be equal members of the tribe. As a result, there are numerous verses in the Quran that, along with the Jewish and Christian scriptures, clearly reflect the subordinate position of women in the male-dominated societies of the ancient world. But that is precisely the point the burgeoning Muslim feminist movement has been making over the last century. These women argue that the religious message of the Quran—a message of revolutionary social egalitarianism—must be separated from the cultural prejudices of seventh-century Arabia. And for the first time in history, they are being given the international audience necessary to incorporate their views into the male-dominated world of Quranic exegesis.

Today, throughout the Muslim world, a new generation of female textual scholars is reengaging the Quran from a perspective that has been sorely lacking in Islamic scholarship. Beginning with the notion that it is not the moral teachings of Islam but the social conditions of seventh-century Arabia and the rampant misogyny of male Quranic exegetes that has been responsible for their inferior status in Muslim society, these women are approaching the Quran free from the confines of traditional gender boundaries. Muslim feminists throughout the world have been laboring toward a more gender-neutral interpretation of the Quran and a more balanced application of Islamic law while at the same time struggling to inject their political and religious views into the male-dominated, conservative societies in which they live. The first English translation of the Quran by a woman, Laleh Bakhtiar, was published in 2009. Muslim feminists do not perceive their cause as a mere social reform movement; they consider it a religious obligation. As Shirin Ebadi proudly declared while accepting the 2003 Nobel Peace Prize for her tireless work in defending the rights of women in Iran, "God created us all as equals. . . . By fighting for equal status, we are doing what God wants us to do."

This Muslim women's movement is based on the idea that Muslim men, not Islam, have been responsible for the suppression of women's rights. For this reason, Muslim feminists throughout the world are advocating a return to the society Muhammad originally envisioned for his followers. Despite differences in culture, nationalities, and beliefs, these women consider that the lesson to be learned from Muhammad in Medina is that Islam is above all an egalitarian religion. Their Medina is a society in which Muhammad designated women like Umm Waraqa as spiritual guides for the Ummah; in which the Prophet himself was sometimes publicly rebuked by his wives; in which women prayed and fought alongside the men; in which women like Aisha and Umm Salamah acted not only as religious but also as political leaders; and in which the call to gather for prayer, bellowed from the rooftop of Muhammad's house, brought men and women together to kneel side by side and be blessed as a single undivided community.

9

The Future of Islam

In the rumbling center of the city of Cairo stands the famed al-Azhar University. For more than a millennium, this mammoth mosque and seminary has served as the locus of Sunni Islamic scholarship. It is the closest thing the Muslim world has to a Vatican. Within its hallowed walls, generations of scriptural scholars (the *Ulama*) have labored to construct a comprehensive code of conduct, the *shariah,* meant to regulate every aspect of the believer's life. There was a time when Muslims from all over the world consulted al-Azhar's revered scholars about everything from how to pray properly to how to properly dispose of fingernail clippings. No longer.

Today, if a Muslim wants legal or spiritual advice on how to live a righteous life, he or she is more likely to pass over the antiquated scholarship of al-Azhar for the televised broadcasts of the wildly popular Muslim televangelist, Amr Khaled. Amr Khaled is not a scholar or a cleric. He has never studied at al-Azhar. In fact, he has never studied Islamic law in any official capacity. Yet through his weekly television program and his popular Web site amrkhaled.net, where he dispenses advice on religious and legal matters to hundreds of millions of Muslims from Jakarta to Detroit, Amr Khaled has taken upon himself the role traditionally reserved for Islam's clerical class as the sole interpreters of the meaning and message of the Muslim faith.

Over the last century, dramatic increases in literacy and education have given Muslims unprecedented access to new ideas and sources of knowledge, even as the rising tide of globalization and the invention of the Internet have made the world a far smaller and more accessible place. The result of all this has been a steady erosion in the religious authority of Islam's traditional clerical institutions as more and more Muslims have begun seizing for themselves the authority, traditionally reserved solely for Islam's clerical class, to define the meaning and message of their faith.

Three major developments in the Muslim world have further accelerated this phenomenon. The first is the unprecedented rate at which the Quran has been translated over the last half-century. Since the end of the seventh century C.E., when its verses were collected and canonized, the Quran has remained fixed in its original Arabic because Islam's clerical institutions insisted that a translation of the holy scripture into any other language would violate the divine nature of the text. To this day, non-Arabic versions of the Quran are considered interpretations of the Quran, not the Quran itself. This means that for most of the last fourteen centuries, some 90 percent of the world's Muslims for whom Arabic is not a primary language had to depend on their clerical leaders to define the meaning and message of the Quran. As one can imagine, such incontestable control over scripture has had a particularly negative effect for Muslim women, who have historically been even further removed from a text whose sole interpreters were, with two or three notable exceptions, strictly men.

But all of that is changing. In the last fifty years, the Quran has been translated into more languages than it had been throughout the previous fourteen centuries. Large numbers of Muslim laity, and especially women, are increasingly brushing aside centuries of traditionalist, male-dominated, and often misogynistic clerical interpretation in favor of an individualized and gender-neutral reading of the Quran. All over the world, Muslims are stripping away centuries of accumulated clerical interpretation in favor of a return to the original founding texts of Islam.

The second development is the rapid influx of Muslim immigrants into Europe and North America. New generations of westernized converts and what are sometimes called veiled-again Muslims (lapsed Muslims who have returned to their faith and traditions in the wake of the attacks of September 11, 2001) are changing the face of global Islam and, in fact, developing what is becoming a whole new kind of Islam, one steeped in rationalism, pluralism, and, above all, individualism.

The third, and perhaps most important, development is, of course, the invention of the Internet, which has made it possible for Muslims to draw upon the opinions not only of their own clerical leaders but also of a host of Muslim activists, academics, and even lay leaders who are propounding fresh and innovative interpretations of Islam, some with messages of peace, others with messages of violence.

All of these developments are having a profound and

lasting effect on how Muslims view and understand their religion. And while it may be too early to tell how such events will change Islam, it is not too difficult to know who will ultimately win the battle between reform and counterreform, between peace and violence, between pluralism and intolerance. When fourteen centuries ago the Prophet Muhammad launched a revolution in Mecca to replace the archaic, rigid, and inequitable strictures of tribal society with a radically new vision of divine morality and social egalitarianism, he tore apart the fabric of traditional Arab society. It took many years of violence and devastation to cleanse the Hijaz of its "false idols." It will take many more to cleanse Islam of its new false idols—bigotry and fanaticism—worshipped by those who have replaced Muhammad's original vision of tolerance and unity with their own ideals of hatred and discord. But while the cleansing may be inevitable, it is up to Muslims themselves, particularly young Muslims, to defend their faith from the ignorance and hatred of others, and thus to help write the next chapter of Islam's story, a story that began fourteen centuries ago, at the end of the sixth century C.E., in the sacred city of Mecca, the land that gave birth to Muhammad ibn Abdallah ibn Abd al-Muttalib: the Prophet and Messenger of God. May peace and blessings be upon him.

Chronology of Key Events

680	Husayn ibn Ali, grandson of the Prophet, killed at Karbala
661–750	The Umayyad Dynasty
750–850	The Abassid Dynasty
756	Last Umayyad prince, Abd al-Rahman, establishes rival Caliphate in Spain
874	The occultation of the Twelfth Imam, or the *Mahdi*
934–1062	Buyid Dynasty rules western Iran, Iraq, and Mesopotamia
969–1171	Fatimid Dynasty rules North Africa, Egypt, and Syria
977–1186	Ghaznavid Dynasty rules Khurasan, Afghanistan, and northern India
1095	Christian Crusades launched by Pope Urban II
1250–1517	Mamluk Dynasty rules Egypt and Syria
1281–1924	The Ottoman Empire
1501–1725	Safavid Dynasty rules Iran
1526–1858	Mughal Dynasty rules India
1857	The Indian Revolt against the British
1924	Creation of secular Turkish republic and the end of the Ottoman Caliphate
1925	Beginning of Pahlavi Dynasty in Iran
1928	The Society of Muslim Brothers founded by Hasan al-Banna in Egypt
1932	Kingdom of Saudi Arabia established
1947	Pakistan founded as first Islamic state
1948	State of Israel established
1952	Free Officers revolt in Egypt, led by Gamal Abd al-Nasser
1979	The Iranian Revolution
1990–91	The Persian Gulf War; al-Qaeda formed
2001	Al-Qaeda attack on New York and Washington

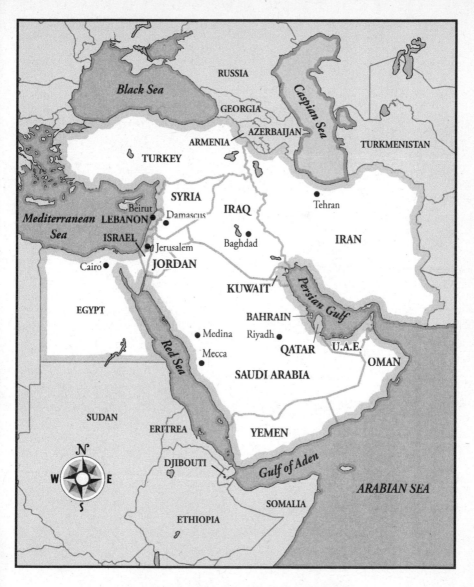

The Arabian Peninsula

Glossary of Key Islamic Terms

ahadiyyah   Meaning "oneness," the Sufi ideal of Divine Unity

ahl/qawm   A people or tribe

ahl al-bayt   The family of the Prophet Muhammad

ahl al-Kitab   The "People of the Book"; usually referring to Jews and Christians (see *dhimmi*)

al-Qaeda   Wahhabist organization headed by Osama bin Laden

amir   A governor of a Muslim province

Ansar   The Helpers; members of Medina's clans who converted to Islam

asbab al-nuzul   The occasions for or causes of a particular verse being revealed to Muhammad

Ash'ari   Traditionalist school of Islamic theology

Ashura   The tenth day of the Islamic month of Muharram and the climax of the Shi'ite mourning ceremonies

Aws   Along with the Khazraj, one of the two main pagan Arab clans in Medina

ayah	A verse of the Quran
ayatollah	Meaning "sign of God"; other than Allamah, the highest level a Shi'ite cleric can achieve
baraka	Spiritual power
Basmallah	Invocation that opens most chapters (Surahs) of the Quran: "In the name of God, the Compassionate, the Merciful"
batin	The implicit, hidden message of the Quran
bay'ah	The oath of allegiance commonly given by the tribe to its Shaykh
bayt/banu	"House/sons," meaning clan
bid'a	Religious innovation
Caliph	The successor to Muhammad and the temporal leader of the Muslim community
Companions	The first generation of Muslims, those who accompanied Muhammad on the Hijra from Mecca to Yathrib (Medina); also called the Muhajirun
darvish	Meaning "beggar," a common term for Sufis
dhikr	Meaning "remembrance," the primary ritual in Sufism
dhimmi	Jews, Christians, and other non-Muslims considered "People of the Book" and protected by Islamic law
du'a	Informal prayer
erfan	Mystical knowledge
fana	The annihilation of the self that occurs when a Sufi has reached a state of spiritual enlightenment
Faqih	A Muslim jurist; the Supreme Leader of Iran
faqir	See *darvish*
fatwa	A legal declaration made by a qualified Muslim jurist
fikr	Mystical contemplation employed by certain Sufi Orders
fiqh	The study of Islamic jurisprudence

fitnah	Muslim civil war
hadith	Stories and anecdotes of the Prophet and his earliest companions
Hajj	The pilgrimage to Mecca
Hakam	An arbiter who settled disputes within and between tribes in pre-Islamic Arabia
Hanif	Pre-Islamic Arab monotheist
Hashim	The name of Muhammad's clan
henotheism	The belief in a single "High God," without the explicit rejection of other, lower gods
hijab	Muslim practice of veiling and seclusion of women
Hijaz	The region of western Arabia
Hijra	The emigration from Mecca to Yathrib (Medina) in 622 C.E.; year 1 A.H. (after Hijra) in the Islamic calendar
Iblis	The Devil (corruption of Latin *diabolus*); Satan
ijma	Traditionally, the consensus of the Ulama on a specific legal issue not covered by the Quran and hadith
ijtihad	The independent legal judgment of a qualified legal scholar, or mujtahid
Ikhwan	The Wahhabist "holy warriors" who helped the Saudis capture Arabia
Imam	In Shi'ism, the divinely inspired leader of the community
Islamism	An Islamic movement whose primary goal is the establishment of an Islamic polity
isnad	A chain of transmission meant to validate individual hadith
Jahiliyyah	The "Time of Ignorance" before the advent of Islam
jihad	A struggle or striving
Jinn	Imperceptible, salvable spirits, known as "genies" in the West

147

jizyah	Protection tax paid by the dhimmi
Ka'ba	The ancient sanctuary at Mecca that housed the tribal deities of the Hijaz before being cleansed by Muhammad and rededicated to Allah
kafir	An unbeliever
Kahin	A soothsayer or ecstatic poet in pre-Islamic Arabia who received inspirations from the Jinn
kalam	Islamic theology
Kharijites	Radical sect that broke off from Shi'ism during Ali's Caliphate
Khazraj	Along with the Aws, one of the two main pagan Arab clans in Medina, and the first clan to accept Muhammad's message
khedive	Egyptian monarchs under the suzerainty of the British Empire
madrassa	Islamic religious school
Mahdi	The "Hidden Imam," who is in occultation until the Last Days, when he will return to usher in a time of justice
matam	Self-flagellation rituals mourning the martyrdom of Husayn
Mujahadin	Muslim militants; literally, "those who wage jihad"
mujtahid	A Muslim jurist worthy of emulation and qualified to make authoritative legal declarations
muruwah	Pre-Islamic code of tribal conduct
Muslim Brothers	Islamic socialist organization founded by Hasan al-Banna in Egypt in 1928
Mu'tazilah	Rationalist school of Islamic theology
nabi	A prophet
nafs	Meaning "breath," the self or ego according to Sufism
Najd	The desert regions of eastern Arabia
naskh	The abrogation of one verse in the Quran by another

148

Pan-Arabism	Principle of racial unity among the world's Arab population
Pan-Islamism	Principle of religious unity among the world's Muslim population
Pir	A Sufi master (also known as Shaykh or Friend of Allah)
Qa'id	Pre-Islamic tribal war leader
qalb	The "heart," corresponding to the soul in Sufism
qiblah	The direction of prayer toward Mecca
qiyas	Analogical reasoning used as a source in the development of Islamic law
Quraysh	The rulers of Mecca in pre-Islamic Arabia
Qurra	The Quran readers who were the first to memorize, record, and disseminate the Revelation
qutb	The "cosmic pole" around which the universe rotates
Rashidun	The first four "Rightly Guided" Caliphs: Abu Bakr, Umar, Uthman, and Ali
rasul	A messenger
ruh	The Universal Spirit; the breath of God
Salafiyyah	Muslim reform movement begun in Egypt by Muhammad Abdu and Jamal ad-Din al-Afghani
salat	Ritual prayer performed five times a day at sunrise, noon, afternoon, sunset, and evening
sawm	Fasting
shahadah	The Muslim profession of faith: "There is no god but God, and Muhammad is God's Messenger."
Shariah	Islamic law whose primary sources are the Quran and hadith
Shaykh	The leader of the tribe or clan; also called Sayyid
Shi'ism	The largest sect in Islam, founded by the followers of Ali

shirk	To obscure the Oneness and Unity of God in any way
shura	A consultative assembly of tribal elders who chose the Shaykh in pre-Islamic Arabia
Sufism	The name given to the mystical traditions in Islam
Sunna	The traditions of the Prophet composed of the hadith
Sunni	The main or "orthodox" branch of Islam
Surah	A chapter of the Quran
Tabiun	The second generation of Muslims after the Companions
tafsir	Traditional Quranic exegesis
tahannuth	Pre-Islamic religious retreat
tajwid	The science of Quranic recitation
tanzil	Direct revelation handed down from God to Muhammad
tariqah	The spiritual path or Way of the Sufi
taqiyyah	Cautionary dissimulation practiced by the Shi'ah
taqlid	Blind acceptance of juridical precedent
tasawwuf	The state of being a Sufi
tawaf	The seven ritual circumambulations of the Ka'ba
tawhid	Meaning "making one," refers to God's Oneness and Unity
ta'wil	Textual exegesis of the Quran that focuses on the hidden, esoteric meaning of the text
ta'ziyeh	A public performance reenacting the martyrdom of Husayn at Karbala
topos	A conventional literary theme
Ulama	Islam's clerical establishment
Ummah	The name given to the Muslim community at Medina
Umm al-Kitab	"The Mother of Books," the heavenly source of all revealed scriptures

umra	The lesser pilgrimage at Mecca
Valayat-e Faqih	"The Guardianship of the Jurist"; the religio-political ideology founded by the Ayatollah Khomeini
Wahhabism	Puritanical sect of Islam founded by Muhammad ibn Abd al-Wahhab in Arabia
wali	The executor of God's divine message
zahir	The explicit message of the Quran
zakat	Mandatory alms given to the Muslim community and distributed to the poor
zakir	Shi'ite religious specialists who recite stories of the martyrs during the Muharram ceremonies
Zamzam	The well situated near the Ka'ba

Works Consulted

Books

Abbott, Nabia. *Studies in Arabic Literary Papyri*. Chicago, 1957–1972.
Abd al-Rahman al-Bazzaz. *Islam and Nationalism*. Baghdad, 1952.
Abedi, Mehdi, and Gary Legenhausen, eds. *Jihad and Shahadat*. Houston, 1986.
Abrahamian, Ervand. *Khomeinism: Essays on the Islamic Republic*. Berkeley, 1993.
Abrahamov, Binyamin. *Islamic Theology: Traditionalism and Rationalism*. Edinburgh, 1998.
Adams, Charles C. *Islam and Modernism in Egypt*. London, 1933.
Ahmad, Barakat. *Muhammad and the Jews: A Re-Examination*. New Delhi, 1979.
Ahmad, Jalal-e. *Gharbzadeghi*. California, 1997.
Ahmed, Leila. *Women and Gender in Islam*. New Haven, 1992.
Ahmed, Rashid. *The Taliban*. New Haven, 2000.
al-Banna, Hasan. *Memoirs of Hasan al-Banna Shaheed*. Karachi, 1981.
Algar, Hamid. *Wahhabism: A Critical Essay*. New York, 2002.
al-Ghazali. *The Alchemy of Happiness*. London, 1980.
———. *The Foundations of the Articles of Faith*. Lahore, 1963.
———. *The Niche of Lights*. Utah, 1998.
———. *The Ninety-nine Beautiful Names of God*. Nigeria, 1970.
al-Rasheed, Madawi. *A History of Saudi Arabia*. Cambridge, 2003.
al-Shaibi, Kamil M. *Sufism and Shi'ism*. Great Britain, 1991.
al-Tabari, Abu Ja'far Muhammad. *The History of al-Tabari*, ed. Ihsan Abbas et al. New York, 1988.

Amin, Osman. *Muhammad 'Abduh*. Washington, D.C., 1953.

Andrae, Tor. *Mohammed: The Man and His Faith*. New York. 1960

Angha, Molana Salaheddin Ali Nader Shah. *The Fragrance of Sufism*. Lanham, 1996.

Angha, Nahid. *Ecstasy*. California, 1998.

———. *Selections*. California, 1991.

An-Na'im, Abdullahi. *Toward an Islamic Reformation*. Syracuse, 1990.

Arjomand, Said Amir. *The Turban for the Crown*. New York, 1988.

Armstrong, Karen. *Muhammad*. San Francisco, 1992.

Asani, Ali and Kamal Abdel-Malek. *Celebrating Muhammad*. South Carolina, 1995.

Ash-Shabrawi, Abd al-Khaliq. *The Degrees of the Soul*. London, 1997.

Attar, Farid ad-Din. *The Conference of the Birds*. New York, 1984.

Badawi, M. A. Zaki. *The Reformers of Egypt*. London, 1979.

Baldick, Julian. *Mystical Islam*. New York, 1989.

Ball, Charles. *The History of the Indian Mutiny*. London, 1860.

Bamyeh, Mohammed A. *The Social Origins of Islam*. Minneapolis, 1999.

Baqer, Moin. *Khomeini: Life of the Ayatollah*. New York, 1999.

Barks, Colman. *The Essential Rumi*. San Francisco, 1995.

Baron, Salo Wittmayer. *A Social and Religious History of the Jews* (3 vols.). New York, 1964.

Bell, Richard. *The Origin of Islam in Its Christian Environment*. London,1968.

Bergen, Peter L. *Holy War, Inc.: Inside the Secret World of Osama bin Laden*. New York. 2001.

Berkey, Jonathan P. *The Formation of Islam*. Cambridge, 2003.

Black, Anthony. *The History of Islamic Political Thought*. New York, 2001.

Boyce, Mary. *History of Zoroastrianism* (3 vols.). Leiden, 1996.

———. *Zoroastrians, Their Religious Beliefs and Practices*. New York, 2001.

Bulliet, Richard. *The Camel and the Wheel*. Cambridge, 1975.

——— *Islam: The View from the Edge*. New York, 1994.

Burckhardt, Titus. *An Introduction to Sufi Doctrine*. Wellingsborough, 1976.

Chelowski, Peter. *Ta'ziyeh: Ritual and Drama in Iran*. New York, 1979.

Cole, Juan R. I. *Colonialism and Revolution in the Middle East*. Princeton, 1993.

Cooper, John, et al., eds. *Islam and Modernity*. London, 1998.

Cooperson, Michael. *Classical Arabic Biography*. Cambridge, 2000.

Cox, Harvey. *The Secular City*. New York, 1966.

Cragg, Kenneth. *The Event of the Qur'an*. Oxford, 1971.

———. *Readings in the Qur'an*. London, 1988.

———. *God's Rule: Government and Islam*. New York, 2004.

Crone, Patricia. *Meccan Trade and the Rise of Islam*. New Jersey, 1987.

——— and M. A. Cook. *Hagarism: The Making of the Islamic World*. Cambridge, 1977.

——— and Martin Hinds. *God's Caliph: Religious Authority in the First Centuries of Islam*. Cambridge, 1986.

Dajani-Shakeel, Hadia, and Ronald A. Messier, eds. *The Jihad and Its Times*. Ann Arbor, 1991.

de Bruijn, J.T.P. *Persian Sufi Poetry*. Surrey, 1997.

de Tocqueville, Alexis. *Democracy in America*. New York, 1969.

Donohue, John J., and John L. Esposito, eds. *Islam in Transition*. New York, 1982.
Doran, Michael. *Pan-Arabism Before Nasser*. Oxford, 1999.
Eliade, Mircea. *The Myth of the Eternal Return*. Princeton, 1954.
———. *The Sacred and the Profane*. San Diego,1959.
Embree, Ainslee. *1857 in India*. Boston, 1963.
Ernst, Carl. *Eternal Garden: Mysticism, History, and Politics at a South Asian Sufi Center*. New York, 1992.
———. *Teachings of Sufism*. Boston, 1999.
Esposito, John L., and John O. Voll. *Makers of Contemporary Islam*. New York, 2001.
Gabrieli, Francesco. *Muhammad and the Conquests of Islam*. New York, 1968.
Gatje, Helmut. *The Qur'an and Its Exegesis*. Berkeley, 1976.
Gelpke, R. *Layla and Majnun*. London, 1966.
Gibb, H.A.R. *Mohammedanism*. London, 1970.
Goiten, S. D. *Jews and Arabs*. New York, 1970.
Goldziher, Ignaz. *Introduction to Islamic Theology and Law*. Princeton, 1981.
———. *Muslim Studies* (2 vols.). Albany, 1977.
Graetz, Heinrich. *History of the Jews* (3 vols.). Philadelphia, 1894.
Griffiths, C. G. *Siege of Delhi*. London, 1912.
Haeri, Shaykh Fadhlalla. *The Elements of Sufism*. Great Britain, 1990.
Haim, Sylvia G., ed. *Arab Nationalism*. Berkeley, 1962.
Halm, Heinz. *Shi'a Islam: From Religion to Revolution*. Princeton, 1997.
Helminski, Camille Adams. *Women of Sufism*. Boston, 2003.
Herberg, Will. *Protestant, Catholic, Jew*. New York, 1955.
Hodgson, Marshall G. S. *The Venture of Islam*. Chicago, 1974.
Hourani, George. *Islamic Rationalism*. Oxford, 1971.
Hoyland, Robert G. *Arabia and the Arabs*. New York, 2001.
Hurvitz, Nimrod. *The Formation of Hanbalism: Piety into Power*. London, 2002.
Ibn Batuta. *The Travels of Ibn Batuta*. Cambridge, 1958.
Ibn Hisham. *The Life of Muhammad*. Oxford, 1955.
Ibn Rushd. *Commentary on Aristotle's Metaphysics*. Leiden, 1984.
———. *The Epistle on the Possibility of Conjunction with the Active Intellect*. New York, 1982.
———. *Three Short Commentaries on Aristotle's "Topics," "Rhetoric," and "Poetics."* Albany, 1977.
Ibn Sina. *The Life of Ibn Sina*. Albany, 1974.
———. *Treatise on Logic*. The Hague, 1971.
Israel, Milton, and N. K. Wagle, eds. *Islamic Societies and Culture: Essays in Honor of Professor Aziz Ahmad*. New Delhi, 1983.
Jafri, S. Husain M. *Origins and Early Development of Shi'a Islam*. London, 1978.
Juynboll, G.H.A., ed. *Studies on the First Century of Islamic Studies*. Carbondale and Edwardsville, Ill., 1982.
Keddie, Nikki R. *Sayyid Jamal al-Din "al-Afghani": A Political Biography*. Berkeley, 1972.
Kelsay, John. *Islam and War*. Kentucky, 1993.
Kepel, Gilles. *Jihad: The Trail of Political Islam*. Cambridge, 2002.
———. *The War for Muslim Minds: Islam and the West*. Cambridge, 2004.

Kerr, Malcolm H. *Islamic Reform: The Political and Legal Theories of Muhammad 'Abduh and Rashid Rida.* Berkeley, 1966.

Khan, Inayat. *The Unity of Religious Ideals.* London, 1929.

Khan, Sayyid Ahmed. *The Causes of the Indian Revolt.* Benares, 1873.

Khomeini, Ruhollah. *A Clarification of Questions.* Boulder, 1984.

———. *Islam and Revolution.* Berkeley, 1981.

———. *Islamic Government.* New York, 1979.

Kochler, Hans. *The Concept of Monotheism in Islam and Christianity.* Austria, 1982.

Lammens, Henri. *Islam: Beliefs and Institutions.* London, 1968.

Lecker, Michael. *Muslims, Jews, and Pagans: Studies on Early Islamic Medina.* Leiden, 1995.

Lings, Martin. *What Is Sufism?* Cambridge, 1993.

Mackey, Sandra. *The Iranians.* New York, 1996.

Madelung, Wilferd. *Religious Schools and Sects in Medieval Islam.* London, 1985.

———. *The Succession to Muhammad.* Cambridge, 1997.

Margoliouth, D. S. *The Relations Between Arabs and Israelites Prior to the Rise of Islam.* London, 1924.

Martin, Richard. *Approaches to Islam in Religious Studies.* Oxford, 2001.

Martin, Richard, et al. *Defenders of Reason in Islam.* Oxford, 1997.

Massignon, Louis. *Essay on the Origins of the Technical Language of Islamic Mysticism.* Bloomington, Ind., 1997.

Mawdudi, Abu-l Ala (Mawlana). *Nationalism and India.* Lahore, 1947.

———. *The Islamic Movement.* London, 1984.

McCarthy, Richard. *The Theology of the Ash'ari.* Beirut, 1953.

Mehr, Farhang. *The Zoroastrian Tradition.* Amherst, Mass., 1991.

Menocal, Maria Rosa. *Ornament of the World.* New York, 2002.

Mernissi, Fatima. *The Veil and the Male Elite.* Cambridge, 1991.

Metcalf, Thomas. *The Aftermath of Revolt.* Princeton, 1964.

Mitchell, Richard P. *Society of the Muslim Brothers.* New York, 1969.

Momen, Moojan. *An Introduction to Shi'i Islam.* New Haven, 1985.

Mottahadeh, Roy. *The Mantle of the Prophet.* New York, 1985.

Naquvi, M. A. *The Tragedy of Karbala.* Princeton, 1992.

Nasr, Seyyed Hossein. *Islamic Art and Spirituality.* New York, 1987.

———. *Sufi Essays.* London, 1972.

Netton, Ian Richard. *Sufi Ritual.* Surrey, 2000.

Newby, Gordon Darnell. *A History of the Jews of Arabia.* South Carolina, 1988.

Nicholson, R. A. *The Mystics of Islam.* London, 1914.

———. *Studies in Islamic Mysticism.* Cambridge, 1921.

Nicholson, Reynolds. *Rumi: Poet and Mystic.* London, 1978.

Nurbakhsh, Javad. *Master and Disciple in Sufism.* Tehran, 1977.

Peters, F. E. *Mecca: A Literary History of the Muslim Holy Land.* New Jersey, 1994.

———. *Muhammad and the Origins of Islam.* New York, 1994.

———. *The Hajj.* New Jersey, 1994.

Peters, Rudolph. *Islam and Colonialism: The Doctrine of Jihad in Modern History.* The Hague, 1979.

————. *Jihad in Classical and Modern Islam.* Princeton,1996.

Pinault, David. *The Horse of Karbala.* New York, 2001.

————. *The Shiites.* New York, 1992.

Pourjavady, Nasrollah, and Peter Wilson. *Kings of Love.* Tehran, 1978.

Qutb, Sayyid. *Milestones.* Indianapolis, 1993.

————. *Social Justice in Islam.* Leiden, 1953.

Rahnema, Ali, ed. *Pioneers of Islamic Revival.* London, 1995.

Rashid, Ahmed. *The Taliban.* New Haven, 2000.

Rejwan, Nissim. *Arabs Face the Modern World.* Florida, 1998.

Renard, John. *Seven Doors to Islam.* Berkeley, 1996.

Robinson, Neal. *Christ in Islam and Christianity.* London, 1991.

Rodinson, Maxime. *Mohammad.* New York, 1971.

Rumi, Jalal al-Din. *Mystical Poems of Rumi* (2 vols.). Chicago, 1968.

————. *Rumi: Poet and Mystic.* London, 1950.

Russell, W. H. *My Indian Diary.* London, 1957.

Sachedina, Abdulaziz Abdulhussein. *Islamic Messianism.* Albany, 1981.

————. *The Islamic Roots of Democratic Pluralism.* Oxford, 2001.

————. *The Just Ruler in Shi'ite Islam.* New York, 1988.

Schacht, Joseph. *An Introduction to Islamic Law.* Oxford, 1998.

————. *Origins of Muhammadan Jurisprudence.* Oxford, 1950.

Schimmel, Annemarie. *And Muhammad Is His Messenger.* Chapel Hill, N.C., 1985.

————. *I Am Wind, You Are Fire: The Life and Works of Rumi.* Boston, 1992.

Schubel, Vernon. *Religious Performance in Contemporary Islam.* Columbia, 1993.

Schwartz, Martin. *Studies on Islam.* New York, 1981.

Sells, Michael. *Desert Tracings: Six Classical Arabian Odes.* Connecticut, 1989.

Shaban, M. A. *Islamic History: A New Interpretation.* Cambridge, 1994.

Shah, Idris. *The Sufis.* New York, 1964.

————. *The Way of the Sufi.* New York, 1969.

Shariati, Ali. *Fatima Is Fatima.* Tehran, 1971.

————. *Iqbal: Manifestations of the Islamic Spirit.* New Mexico, 1991.

Smith, Margaret. *Rabi'a the Mystic and Her Fellow-Saints in Islam.* Cambridge, 1928.

Smith, Wilfred Cantwell. *Islam in Modern History.* Princeton, 1957.

Soroush, Abdolkarim. *Reason, Freedom, and Democracy.* New York, 2000.

Stillman, Norman A. *The Jews of Arab Lands.* Philadelphia, 1979.

Tabataba'i, Muhammad H. *Qur'an in Islam.* London, 1988.

————. *Shi'ite Islam.* New York, 1979.

Taha, Mahmoud. *The Second Message of Islam.* Syracuse, 1987.

Thompson, Edward J. *The Other Side of the Medal.* London, 1925.

Trevelyan, C. E. *On the Education of the People of India.* Hyderabad, 1838.

Trimingham, J. Spencer. *The Sufi Orders in Islam.* Oxford, 1971.

Troll, Christian W. *Sayyid Ahmed Khan: A Reinterpretation of Muslim Theology.* New Delhi, 1978.

Turner, Bryan S. *Weber and Islam: A Critical Study.* London, 1974.

Von Denffer, Ahmad. *Ulum al-Quran: An Introduction to the Sciences of the Qur'an.* Leicester, 1983.

Wadud, Amina. *Quran and Woman: Rereading the Sacred Text from a Woman's Perspective.* New York, 1999.

Walzer, Michael. *Just and Unjust Wars.* New York, 1977.

Wansbrough, John. *Quranic Studies: Sources and Methods of Scriptural Interpretation.* Oxford, 1977.

———. *The Sectarian Milieu: Content and Composition of Islamic Salvation History.* Oxford, 1978.

Watt, W. Montgomery. *The Faith and Practice of al-Ghazali.* London, 1953.

———. *Islamic Creeds.* Edinburgh, 1994.

———. *Islamic Political Thought.* Edinburgh, 1968.

———. *Muhammad at Mecca.* London, 1953.

———. *Muhammad at Medina.* Oxford, 1956.

———. *Muhammad: Prophet and Statesman.* London, 1961.

Welch, William M. *No Country for a Gentleman.* New York, 1988.

Wolfson, Harry Austryn. *The Philosophy of Kalam.* Cambridge, 1976.

Zabiri, Kate. *Mahmud Shaltut and Islamic Modernism.* New York, 1993.

Zaheri, Dariush. *The Iranian Revolution: Then and Now.* Boulder, Colo., 2000.

Zakaria, Rafiq. *The Struggle Within Islam: The Conflict Between Religion and Politics.* London, 1989.

Zawati, Hilmi M. *Is Jihad a Just War?* Lewiston, Me., 2001.

Articles

Abbot, Freedland. "The Jihad of Sayyid Ahmad Shahid," *Muslim World* (1962) 216–22.

al-Faruqi, Lois Ibsen. "The Cantillation of the Qur'an," *Asian Music* 19:1 (1987) 2–23.

Arafat, W. N. "New Light on the Story of Banu Qurayza and the Jews of Medina," *Journal of the Royal Asiatic Society* (1976) 100–107.

Aslan, Reza. "The Problem of Stoning in the Islamic Penal Code: An Argument for Reform," *Journal of Islamic & Near Eastern Law* 3 (2004).

———. "Thus Sprang Zarathustra: A Brief Historiography on the Date of the Prophet of Zoroastrianism," *Jusur: Journal of Middle Eastern Studies* 14 (1998–99) 21–34.

Caetani, Leone. "Uthman and the Recension of the Koran," *The Muslim World* 5 (1915) 380–90.

Conrad, Lawrence I. "Abraha and Muhammad," *Bulletin of the School of Oriental and African Studies* 50 (1987) 225–40.

Gil, Moshe. "The Constitution of Medina: A Reconsideration," *Israel Oriental Studies* 6 (1974) 44–65.

———. "The Medinan Opposition to the Prophet," *Jerusalem Studies in Arabic and Islam* 10 (1987) 65–96.

———. "Origin of the Jews of Yathrib," *Jerusalem Studies in Arabic and Islam* 4 (1984) 203–24.

Guillaume, Alfred. "New Light on the Life of Muhammad," *Journal of Semitic Studies* (1960) 27–59.

Halperin, David. "The Ibn Sayyad Traditions and the Legend of al-Dajjal," *Journal of the American Oriental Society* 96 (1976) 213–25.

Hawting, G. R. "We Were Not Ordered with Entering It but Only with Circumambulating It: *Hadith* and *Fiqh* on Entering the Kaaba," *Bulletin of the School of Oriental and African Studies* 47 (1984) 228–42.

Huntington, Samuel. "The Clash of Civilizations," *Foreign Affairs* 72:3 (Summer 1993) 22–49.

Kister, M. J. "*al-Tahannuth:* An Inquiry into the Meaning of a Term," *Bulletin of the School of Oriental and African Studies* 30 (1968) 223–36.

———. " 'A Bag of Meat:' A Study of an Early Hadith," *Bulletin of the School of Oriental and African Studies* 31 (1968) 267–75.

———. "Do Not Assimilate Yourselves . . . ," *Jerusalem Studies in Arabic and Islam* 12 (1989) 321–71.

———. "The Market of the Prophet," *Journal of the Economic and Social History of the Orient* 8 (1965) 272–76.

———. "The Massacre of the Banu Qurayza: A Reexamination of a Tradition," *Jerusalem Studies in Arabic and Islam* 8 (1986) 61–96.

Nelson, Kristina. "Reciter and Listener: Some Factors Shaping the Mujawwad Style of Qur'anic Reciting," *Ethnomusicology* (Spring/Summer 1987) 41–47.

Rahman, Hannah. "The Conflicts Between the Prophet and the Opposition in Medina," *Der Islam* 62 (1985) 260–97.

Reissener, H. G. "The Ummi Prophet and the Banu Israil," *The Muslim World* 39 (1949).

Rubin, Uri. "Hanafiyya and Ka'ba: An Enquiry into the Arabian Pre-Islamic Background of *din Ibrahim*," *Jerusalem Studies in Arabic and Islam* 13 (1990) 85–112.

———. "The Ka'ba: Aspects of Its Ritual Function and Position in Pre-Islamic and Early Times," *Jerusalem Studies in Arabic and Islam* 8 (1986) 97–131.

Select Dictionaries and Encyclopedias

A Dictionary of Buddhism. Damien Keown, ed. Oxford, 2003.

The Encyclopedia of Gods. Michael Jordan, ed. Great Britain, 1992.

The Encyclopedia of Indo-European Culture. J. P. Mallory and D. Q. Adams, eds. New York, 1997.

The Encyclopedia of Islam (11 vols.). H.A.R. Gibb et al., eds. Leiden, 1986.

The Encyclopedia of Religion (16 vols.). Mircea Eliade et al., eds. New York, 1987.

The Encyclopedia of World Mythology and Legend. Anthony S. Mercatante, ed. New York, 1988.

The Encyclopedia of World Religions. Wendy Doniger, ed. Springfield, Mass., 1999.

The New Encyclopedia of Islam. Cyril Glasse, ed. Walnut Creek, Calif., 2002.

The Oxford Dictionary of World Religions. John Bowker, ed. Oxford, 1997.

The Oxford Encyclopedia of the Modern Islamic World. John L. Esposito, ed. Oxford, 1995.

Index

161

163

166

About the Author

Reza Aslan has studied religions at Santa Clara University, Harvard University, and the University of California, Santa Barbara. He holds an MFA in fiction from the Writers' Workshop at the University of Iowa, where he was named the Truman Capote Fellow in fiction. The adult edition of *No god but God* was listed by Blackwell Publishers as one of the hundred most important books of the past decade. Reza Aslan is also the editor of *Tablet & Pen: Literary Landscapes from the Modern Middle East,* an anthology of twentieth-century Middle Eastern literature. Born in Iran, Reza Aslan now lives in Los Angeles, where he is associate professor of creative writing at UC Riverside.